The Magic Mesh
Mosaic Mesh Projects

Sigalit Eshet

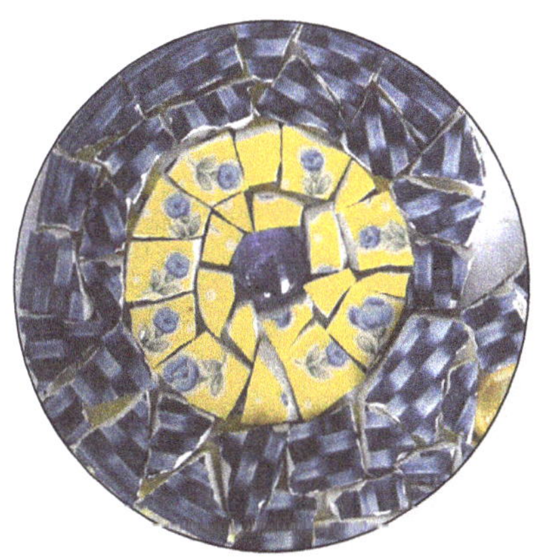

First Print Edition: 2015

Disclaimer

All do-it-yourself activities involve risk, and your safety is your own responsibility, including proper use of equipment and safety gear, and determining whether you have adequate skill and experience.

Some of the resources used for these projects are dangerous unless used properly and with adequate pre-cautions, including safety gear.

Some illustrative photos do not depict safety precautions or equipment, in order to show the project step more clearly.

Some projects are user-submitted, and appearance of a project in this format does not indicate it has been checked for safety or functionality. Use of the instructions and suggestions is at your own risk.

I disclaim all responsibility for any resulting damage, injury, or expense. It is your responsibility to make sure that your activities comply with all applicable laws.

ISBN: 978-965-92633-0-1

www.sigalitart.net/en

Publisher: Simple Story
www.simplestory.us

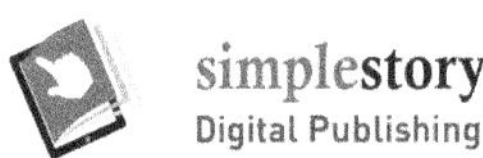

Content:

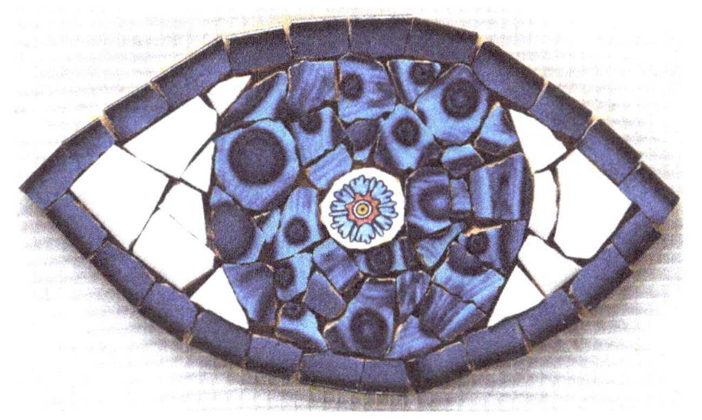

Introduction:

There are many methods for making mosaics. After learning some, you can choose the most appropriate way for you. The mosaic art combine different materials, shapes, cutting styles, designs, and bases.

In this book, which is the sixth in a series of my mosaic books (kindle versiln), I decided to focus on mosaic mesh projects.

Why Mesh?

Lately, I have noticed that my students really love working on mesh. They decorate their house walls this way, especially outside walls. The results are beautiful and colorful. I decided to share my knowledge with you. In this book, you will find many examples of mosaic mesh work that you can use to decorate your house walls - inside or outside.

One of the uses of the mesh is as a secondary preparation station, when the original preparation location for the mosaic work is too far from the installation area. The flexibility of the mesh allows us to make the mosaic work at home or in the studio, then we can easily pack (also in separate parts) it up and stick it in the appropriate place. The mesh is easy to cut so you can create different forms of mosaic art work, not just straight, like cutout. Much easier than cutting a complex shape in boards, with a saw.

Here are some examples of mosaic works that include mesh as a base:

- Stairs
- Name, letters, and house numbers
- Uneven shapes
- Bathroom tiles
- Pictures you want to copy (and put behind the mesh)
- A big wall image that is divided into parts
- Joint Group working

In this book we will learn two techniques of mosaic on mesh. The first one is sticking pieces directly on the mesh, and the second is a mesh base that we will make.

The difference between the two methods is the type of glue used and in the grout making.

My name is Sigalit Eshet. I'm a mosaic artist, and I have taught mosaics for several years. In my studio, I create and teach mosaic and believe that any person can find a way to express him or herself through it. I studied Art and teaching Art in University, and I have worked as a graphic designer for many years. I have specialized in many different fields of art over the years, and I combine all my experience to create my mosaic work.

When making mosaic wall picture, the mesh work is very suitable for use with broken plates or cups. Later in this book you will see many examples. This is the time to collect all the unused or broken dishes you have, search in flea markets for special and colorful plates that you can break, tell all your neighbors to gather some for you ... and start your mosaic mesh work.

There is a bonus for you. All the patterns that are showed in this book, are available in a pdf file, for your use:

Just type **http://goo.gl/ykzw2y** in your browser and get it.

Be creative and use your imagination,

Sigalit Eshet

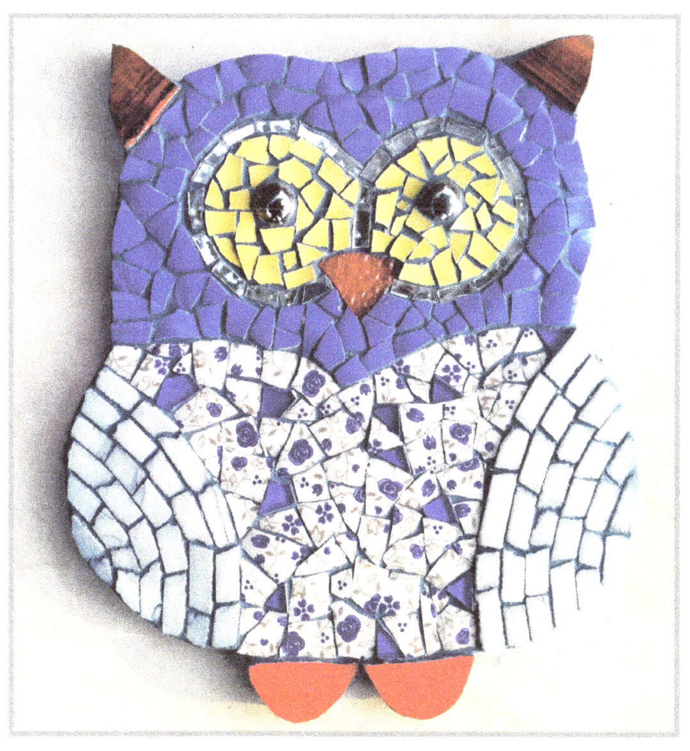

Mosaic Materials

When you make a mosaic mesh work, the materials can be varied and depend on the type of work you are making.

If it's any wall picture, you can mix different types of materials with different heights. When combining tiles with glasses and plates, beads and found objects in one work, the mosaic work is much more interesting and rich.

If you make a floor mat, for example, it is very important that the surface will be smooth and therefore you should use tiles with the same height.

Mosaic materials are varied and include:

Colorful ceramic tiles – You can find them in different shapes and sizes.

Glass tiles – These come in uniform size squares and in many colors. They have one smooth flat side (which should face up), and a rough side (face down; this is the side to which glue is applied).

Stained glass – You can get this in many colors and textures. You can cut it with a nipper or a glass cutter.

Ceramic square tiles – These are available in many colors, textures, and shapes. They come mostly on a square mesh.

China and crockery – Using proper safety precautions, these can be broken or used to cut your own tiles from. Something you get from plates is the unique texture that you can't find in tiles.

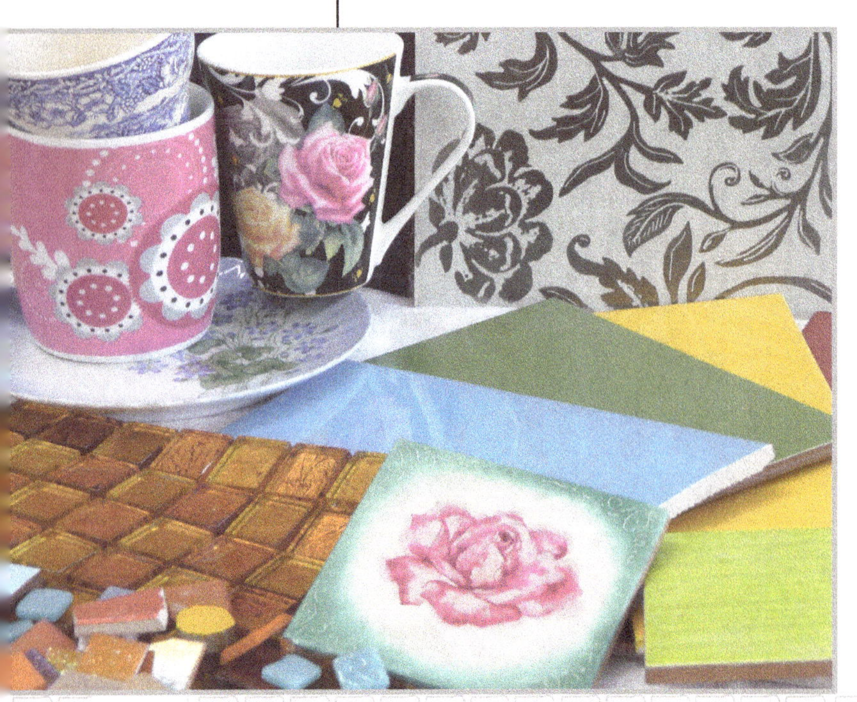

Found objects – These include: beads, seashells, glass beads, buttons, glass nuggets, necklaces, or brooches. Use it to decorate and enrich your work.

Mirrors –These can add a beautiful reflective touch to any mosaic piece.

Polymer clay – Use polymer clay, like Fimo, to decorate your mosaic work.

Mosaic tools and equipment

Basic mosaic tools are inexpensive and easily attainable (in the list below I also included some materials for advanced use):

Safety equipment:

Safety goggles – to protect your eyes from ceramic fragments. Use it when you cut the ceramic.

Dust mask – use this when making the grout.

Preparation tools

Pencil – for drawing the desired pattern on the substrate material.

Ruler – to mark straight lines.

Latex gloves – to protect your hands from scratches and dirt.

Rubber gloves – put these on before you start working with grout.

Plastic tools – for grout mixing, tile collecting and gluing.

Small brush – for cleaning the surface from dust and small particles.

Thin screwdriver – for cleaning tile adhesive residue.

Tweezers – for the placement of small parts.

Paintbrush – for adhesive application.

Wooden mixing sticks – for mixing grout and applying the tile adhesive.

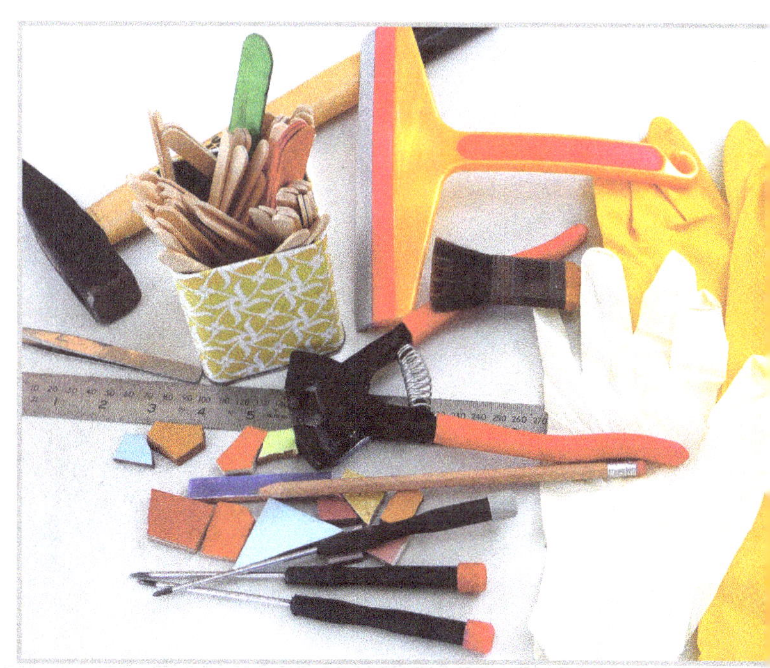

Cutting Tools

Mosaic tile cutter – for cutting and grinding ceramic tiles. You can get these in hardware stores.

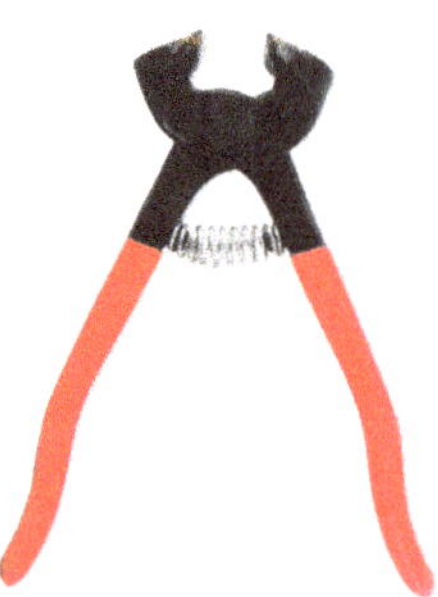

Using the mosaic cutter

1. Before cutting put Safety goggles to protect your eyes from small fragments.

2. Hold the bottom of the cutter with your dominant hand with the curved side facing toward the ceramics. Hold the ceramic tile in your non-dominant hand, and in your dominant hand, hold the bottom of the cutter handle.

3. Hold the ceramic tile with the cutter in a straight or diagonal direction to suit the type of crop you want, and clip!

Tip: If it's your first time, start with cutting soft ceramic tiles for easy use. In time, you can try to cut different kinds of tiles.

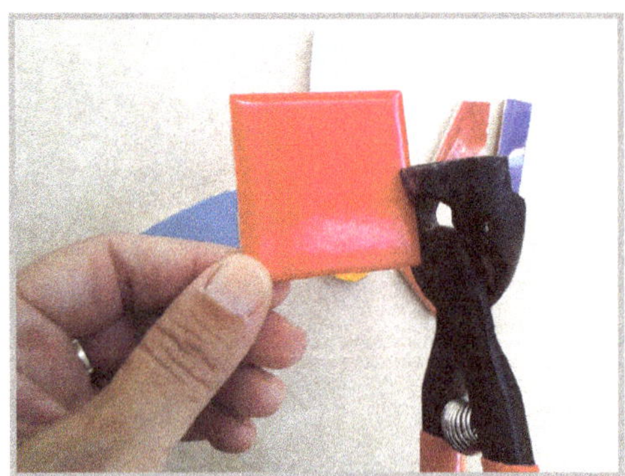

Wheeled glass nipper – for cutting glass, China and crockery.

Using the mosaic Nipper

1. Before cutting put Safety goggles to protect your eyes from small fragments.

2. Hold the bottom of the nipper with your dominant hand with the wheels facing toward the glass. Hold the glass in your non-dominant hand, and in your dominant hand, hold the bottom of the nipper handle.

3. Clip to cut. You can cut with the nipper round or straight shapes.

4. You can cut with the nipper china, cups and crockery.

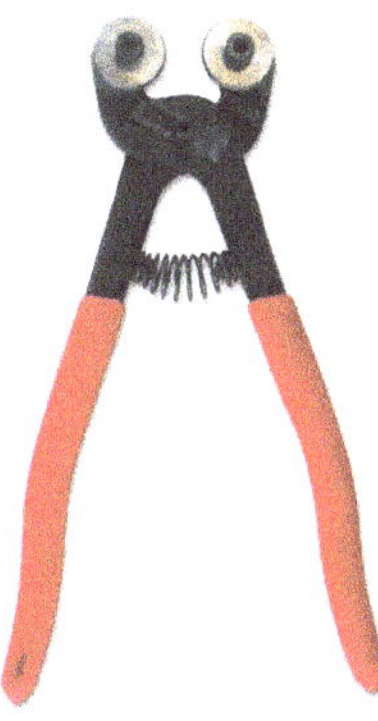

Ceramic cutting machine – for advanced cutters, used to cut ceramic into straight and accurate tiles.

Hammer – for cutting thick ceramic, or when you want to cut random shapes. Please note that when you cut ceramic with a hammer, you should wrap the ceramic with an old towel and place it on top of a thick wood or metal surface.

Tip: Another way to cut a plate is to put it between too towels and beat with a hammer. Use this way only if you don't bother what shape the parts will be.

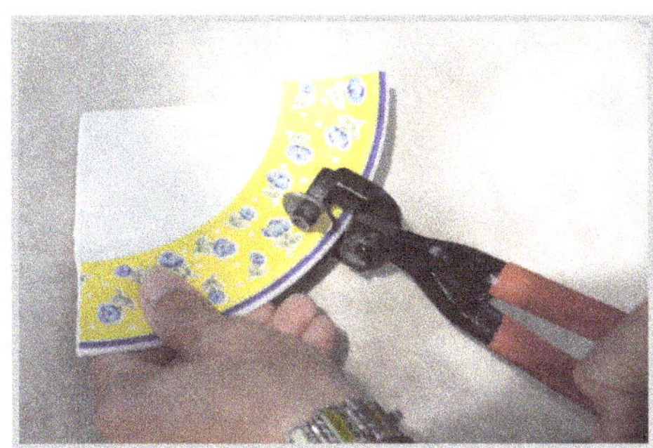

The Mesh

There are several types of mesh suitable for the mosaic work.

In this book we will use two kinds of fiberglass mesh - thick and thin. You can find it at building supply stores. Buy it in the needed length, as you buy fabric.

Most of the mesh mosaic works are made on the medium fiberglass mesh.

The special technique we will learn combines two kinds of mesh in one work.

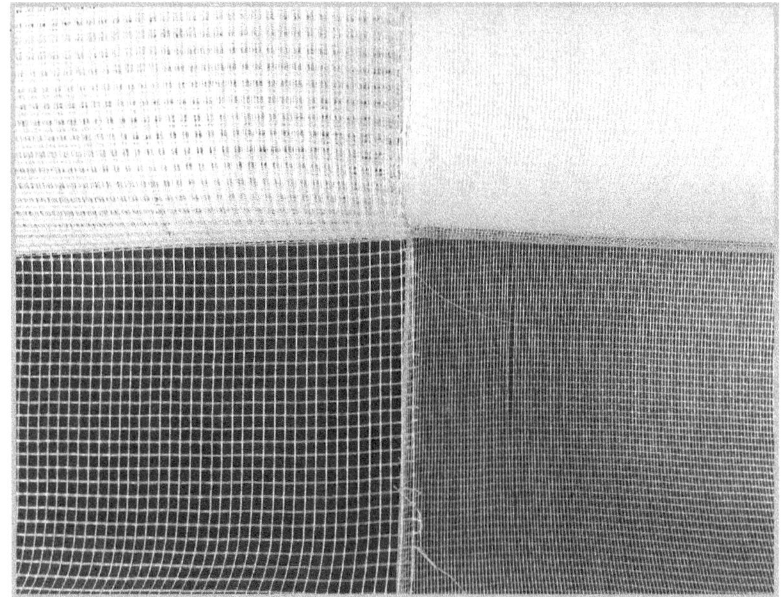

Adhesives

On the fiberglass mesh stick your mosaic work with **PVA white glue** or **carpenter's wood glue**.

Use the appropriate kind for you – there is a wide range of this glue in many kinds of bottles and prices.

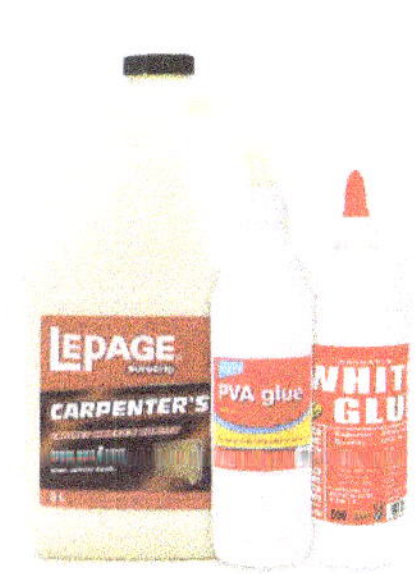

After drying, this adhesive holds well our mosaic on the mesh until connecting to the appropriate place.

Please note: Do not to put too much glue when gluing on the mesh, we want to remain a place for the tile adhesive to get between the mesh slots when staking the mosaic to it's place.

Other adhesives will be used for gluing the mosaic to the wall:

- Mosaic outdoor tile adhesive - A highly flexible, water-resistant, non-slip, ready mixed ceramic wall tile adhesive designed for use in internal wet and dry areas. It comes in big packages and you can find it in any hardware store.

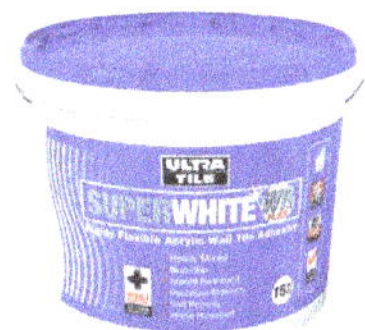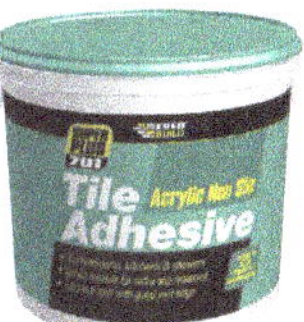

- Strong silicone adhesive like super 7 - a gel like adhesive, available in white or clear. Better to use with a caulking gun. Dried very quickly, very good to use with vertical applications.

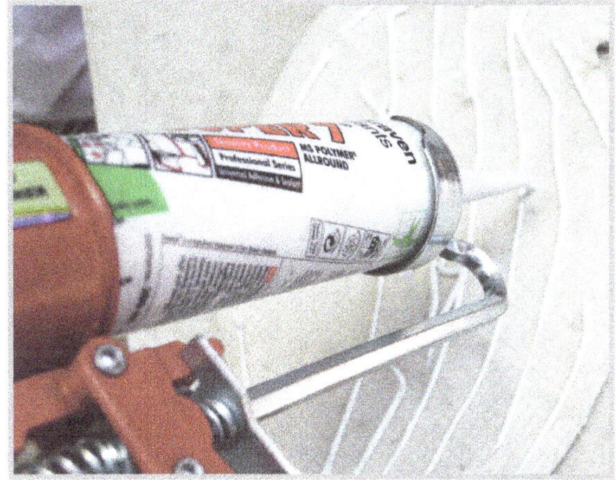

Grout

Grout – to fill the gaps between the tiles.

NOTE: There are different types of grout. Most of them come in powdered form, which you will need to mix with water according the manufacturer's instructions. Grout also comes in different colors, so choose the right color for your work. You can also mix acrylic paint into white grout to make your own custom colored grout, but if you do this, be sure that the final work is not exposed to the sun or water.

Working with the grout can be messy, so wear appropriate clothing and put on gloves before you begin.

Water – for making grout and cleaning.

Small squeegee – for gripping and putting the grout on straight surfaces.

Sponge or cotton rags – for grout cleaning.

Old newspapers – to put under your work to maintain a clean work surface.

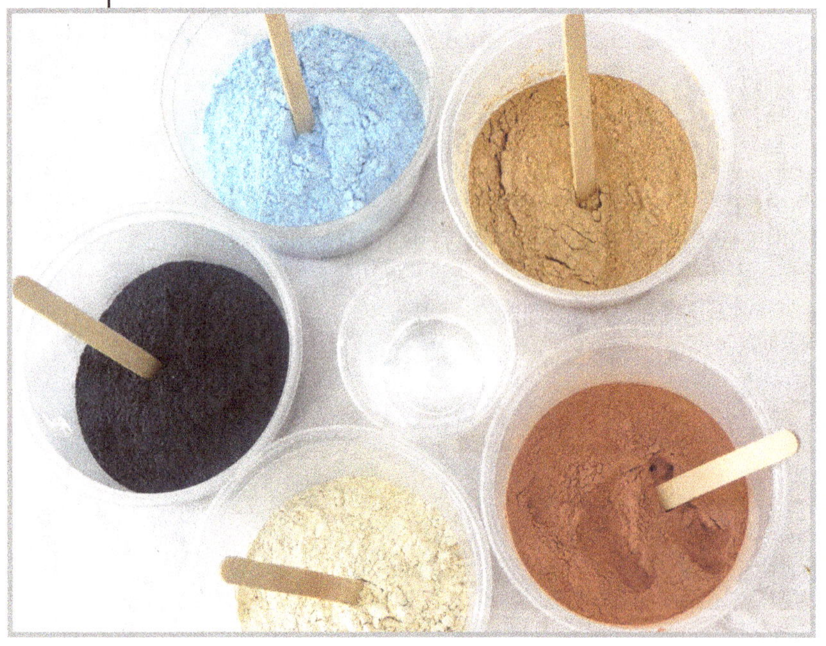

Grout used to fill the gaps between tiles. In mosaic work, the grout is used as finishing method. It is used to fill the spaces between the cut tiles. In addition, it strengthens the work and unites all the parts to create a whole piece of work. The grout moderates the differences in height between the cut tiles and slides the mosaic work.

The grout is available in white or various other colors. White grout can blend easily with acrylic or color pigments, in cases where the work stays at home.

Choosing grout color: You can use an opposite color, to emphasis your work – in this case, a dark gray will be a great choice. You can use a color that blends with your design. In any case – don't try to fix the grout color when the work is done. Even if you don't like it, you will have to just live with it!

In the direct mesh work, make the grout on the wall, after the mosaic work is affixed to it.

In the second technique, which we created the working surface, we will make the grout as any other flat mosaic work, on our desk, in a balanced way. We will attach the finished work directly to the wall.

The grouting stages are almost the same in both techniques.

Applying a grout - step by step:

1. Wear a dust mask to protect your face.

2. Put grout into a plastic bowl, in the appropriate quantity and color. In time, your experience will teach you about the appropriate amount. If there's not enough grout, remix grout + water, in the same bowl.

3. Pour water in the grout bowl. Mix with a wooden stick until the texture is like a cream. Note the manufacturer's instructions.

4. Put on your rubber gloves.

5. If necessary, put old newspapers under your work

6. If there are parts of the substrate you do not want to get dirty, they must be protected with painter's tape before grouting.

7. Apply the grout: on a flat surface, use a small squeegee and spread the grout on the surface until it fills in all slots and holes. On walls, spread the grout by hand and stuff it into the holes between the tiles.

8. After a few minutes, when the grout starts to dry, start cleaning: wet the surface using a clean cotton rag or a sponge. Use a wet and dry rag several times until the work is clean.

   IMPORTANT: Make sure to wet the work. Wetting the grout makes it harder and prevents cracks. Don't skip this step!

9. If revealed "holes" after cleaning, fill with grout, let it dry and clean until you get a smooth and clean work.

10. Adhesive residue can be cleaned with wooden skewer or a thin screwdriver.

11. At the end of the work you can be polish it with a wet wipe.

12. If some tile falls during grouting, clean the place well. Wait until the end of grouting process and then glue the fallen part (you can use speed glue), wait for completely drying and fill the holes with grout.

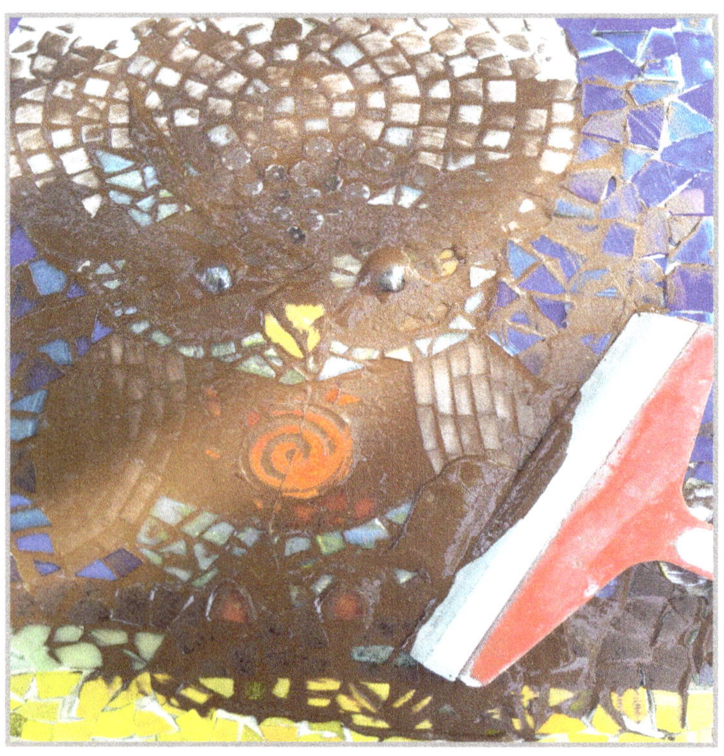

Mosaic on Mesh - Direct Adhesion

In this book, we will learn two methods for gluing mosaic on fiberglass mesh.

When it comes to small mosaic artwork, you have to decide which method to use. You should study the advantages and disadvantages of each method and see what suits you, based on the kind of work you are going to make.

Let's start with the direct method of gluing the mosaic on the mesh itself.

Advantages:

1. If you glue directly on the mesh it is easy to do with white PVA glue, which is very easy material to work with.

2. Samples can be copied easily – just put a painted or painted paper below the mesh.

3. It is possible to create surfaces in any form you choose.

4. This method appropriate also to very large mosaic works – in this case the mesh can be divided into parts and gather together when installing the mosaic in the final place.

5. Easy transport: you can create your mosaic work in one place, roll, pack and paste elsewhere

Disadvantages:

1. You have to do the grout on the wall itself, and sometimes it is hard and difficult work. The access not always easy, and this makes the grout work awkward, especially when you have to stand for several hours on a ladder to reach the mosaic final place.

2. It you stick your mosaic on a wall, you have to keep the surface around your mosaic piece clean in the grouting process. It is hard when the wall isn't smooth.

Working method:

1. Print the desired mosaic pattern in the appropriate size and put it on a flat working surface, preferably on wood panel / large tile or table it can stay there until the end.

2. Cover the paper with transparent plastic sheet, a little bit larger than the printed page. After the work is drying you can easily peel off the plastic from the mesh – the glue does not stick to it.

3. Cover the clear plastic with fiberglass mesh, slightly larger from your design.

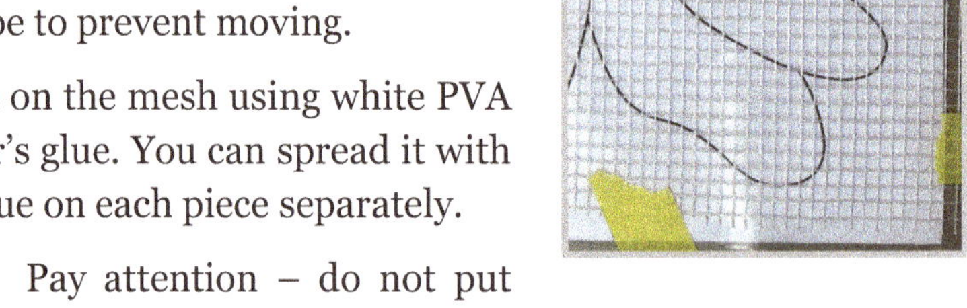

4. Tape everything together on the surface work with masking tape to prevent moving.

5. Paste the mosaic on the mesh using white PVA glue or carpenter's glue. You can spread it with a brush or put glue on each piece separately.

6. Pay attention – do not put too much glue on the mesh – the mesh slots have to remain available to receive the adhesive tile below when pasting if to the wall.

7. After completion of gluing the mosaic you have to wait several hours for drying.

8. Turn the mosaic, remove the plastic and wait for drying.

9. Cut the mesh around the mosaic closely and accurately with cutting knife or scissors.

10. Allow to set for at least 24 hours.

11. Pasting: on the back side of your mosaic work spread adhesive tile or strong acrylic mastic. Always follow the manufacturer's directions. Note that the work is not sliding down while installing. Hold and push the piece to the place. Keep doing until every mosaic piece is stuck to place.

12. Clean adhesive residue around with screwdriver, small stick or rag.

13. Wait at least 24 hours and grout – see grout instructions.

14. Keep your working surface clean. Clean with a wet rag or trowel the residue grout around your work.

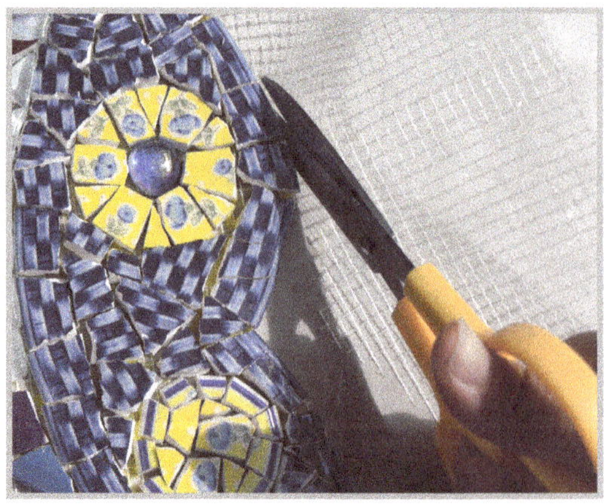

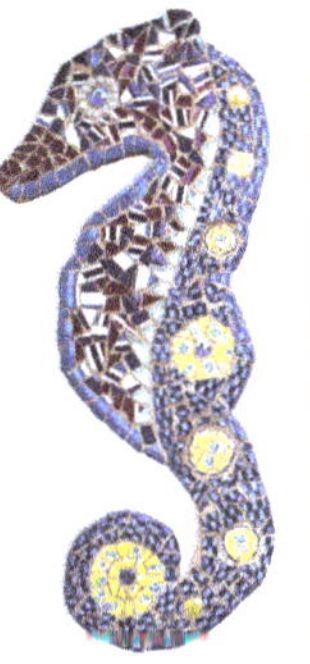

Project: Seahorse

This nice seahorse is made from materials that you can find in every house - some broken plates, beads, some round clear glass. Select especially colorful plates and adjust the colors by your personal taste. You can of course paste tiles instead of plates.

You will need:

Fiberglass mesh cut to the desire size (The original pattern size is 57 cm / 22.2" high)

Clear plastic, a little bit longer than the mesh

Masking tape

Small brush

White glue or carpenter's glue

Outdoor tile adhesive

Trowel

Mosaic Nipper

Colorful plates

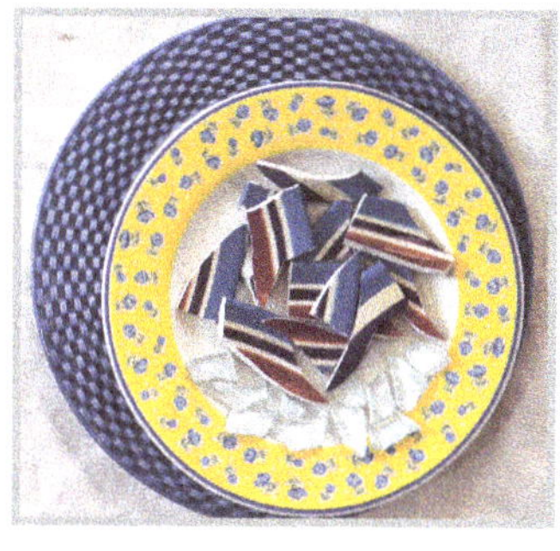

White beads

Some round clear glass

Light brown grout

Grout Equipment: mixing bowl, water, a wooden stick, rags, gloves, Small squeegee and dust mask

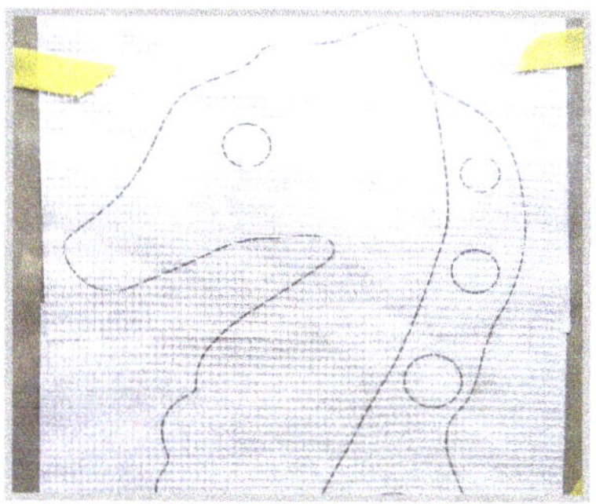

1 Print the seahorse pattern in the desired size.

2 Use the masking-tape to paste together the printed paper, clear plastic and mesh on the working surface.

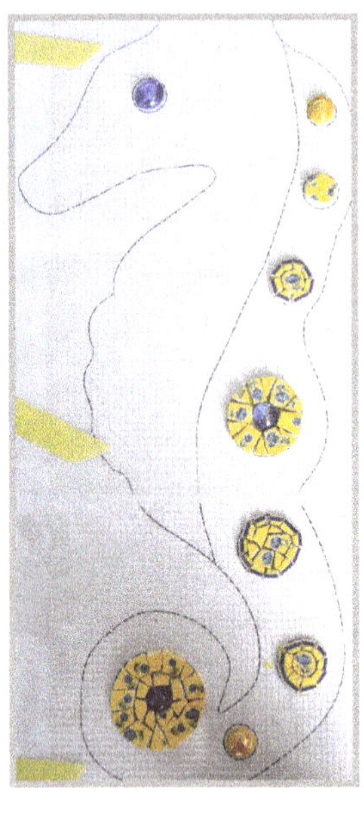

3 Prepare the mosaic materials: pre-cut all the materials and sort them by types in separate tools to make your work easy. This work mainly used colored plates.

4 Start from creating circles in the seahorse's body – in the big circles pasted one round clear glass in the center. Surround it with fragments of cut plates to create a circle.

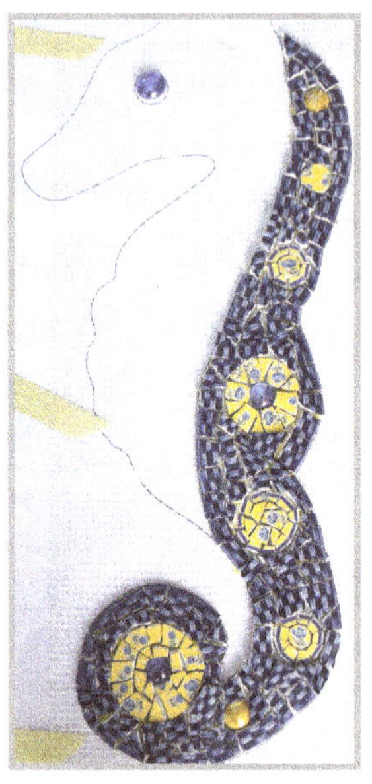

5 Fill the circles background all over the seahorse with one type of plate fragments.

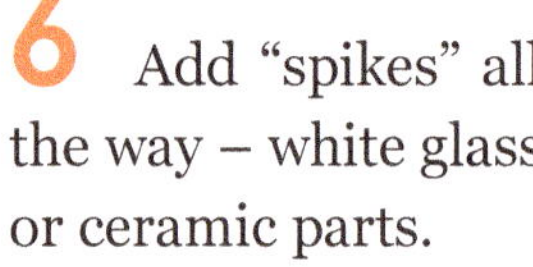

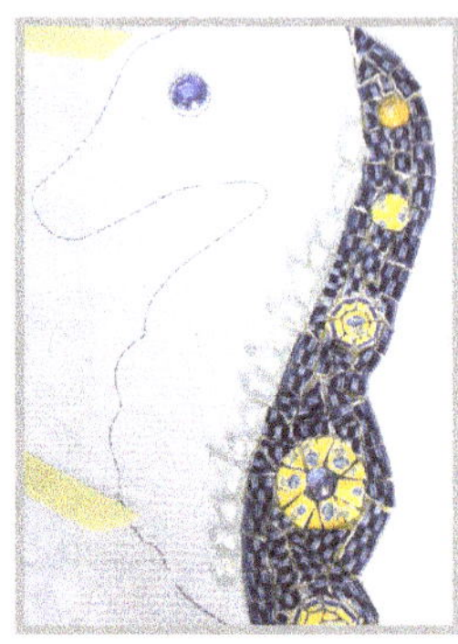

6 Add "spikes" all the way – white glass or ceramic parts.

7 Add one round blue clear glass for the eye and white beads around it.

8 Emphasize the ear with black ceramic triangles or glass triangles.

9 Complete the seahorse body with a different color of a broken plate. Make contour with a different color.

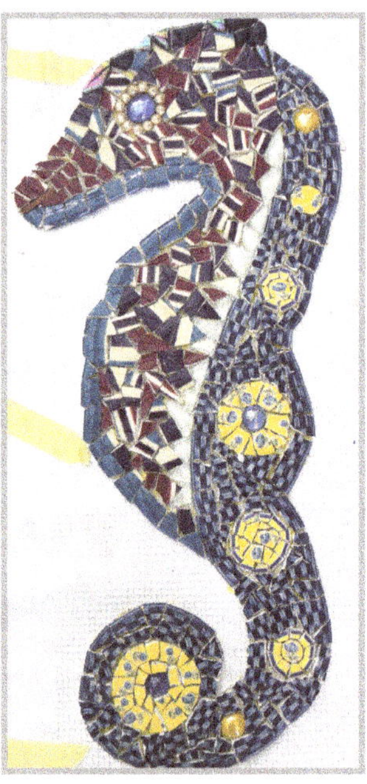

10 Dry, remove the plastic and dry again. Cut the mesh with scissors or knife.

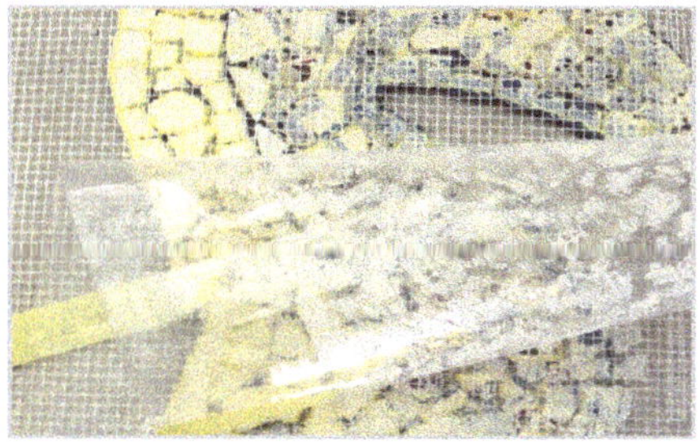

11 Prepare the wall pasting surface - make sure that the place is clean, smooth slightly if necessary.

12 Spread tile adhesive with a Trowel on the seahorse's back side and push it hard to the wall.

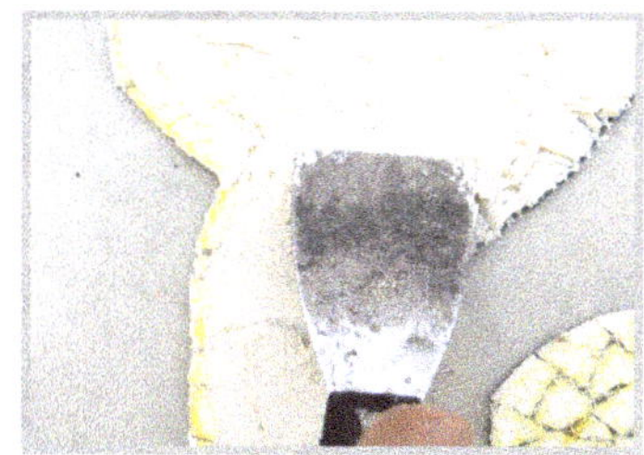

13 Compress all the tiles to the wall, this also will strengthen the adhesion and remove the spare glue out.

14 With a thin screwdriver remove spare adhesive before everything dries.

15 Let it dry for at least 24 hours, grout according to grout instructions.

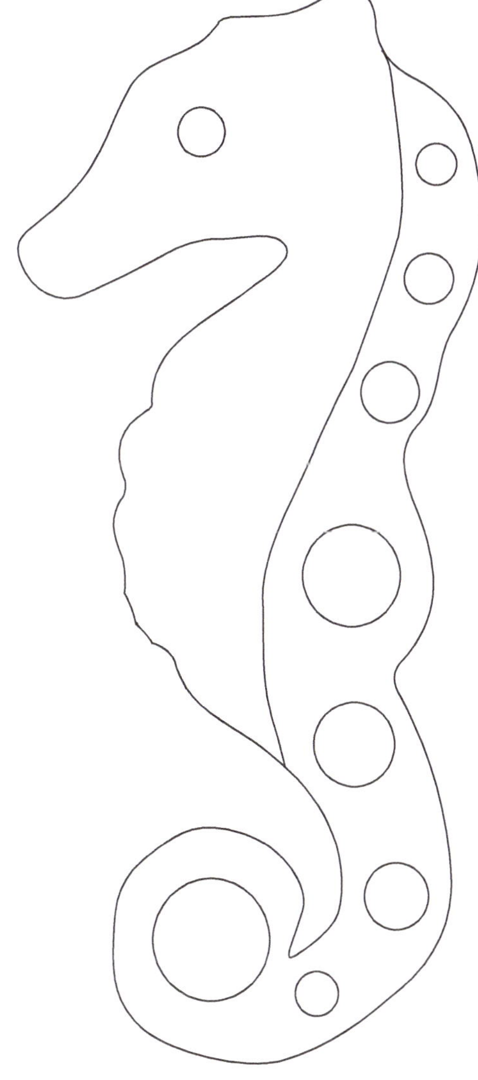

Pattern for the Seahorse:
Enlarge on a photocopier by 410% for a full size design

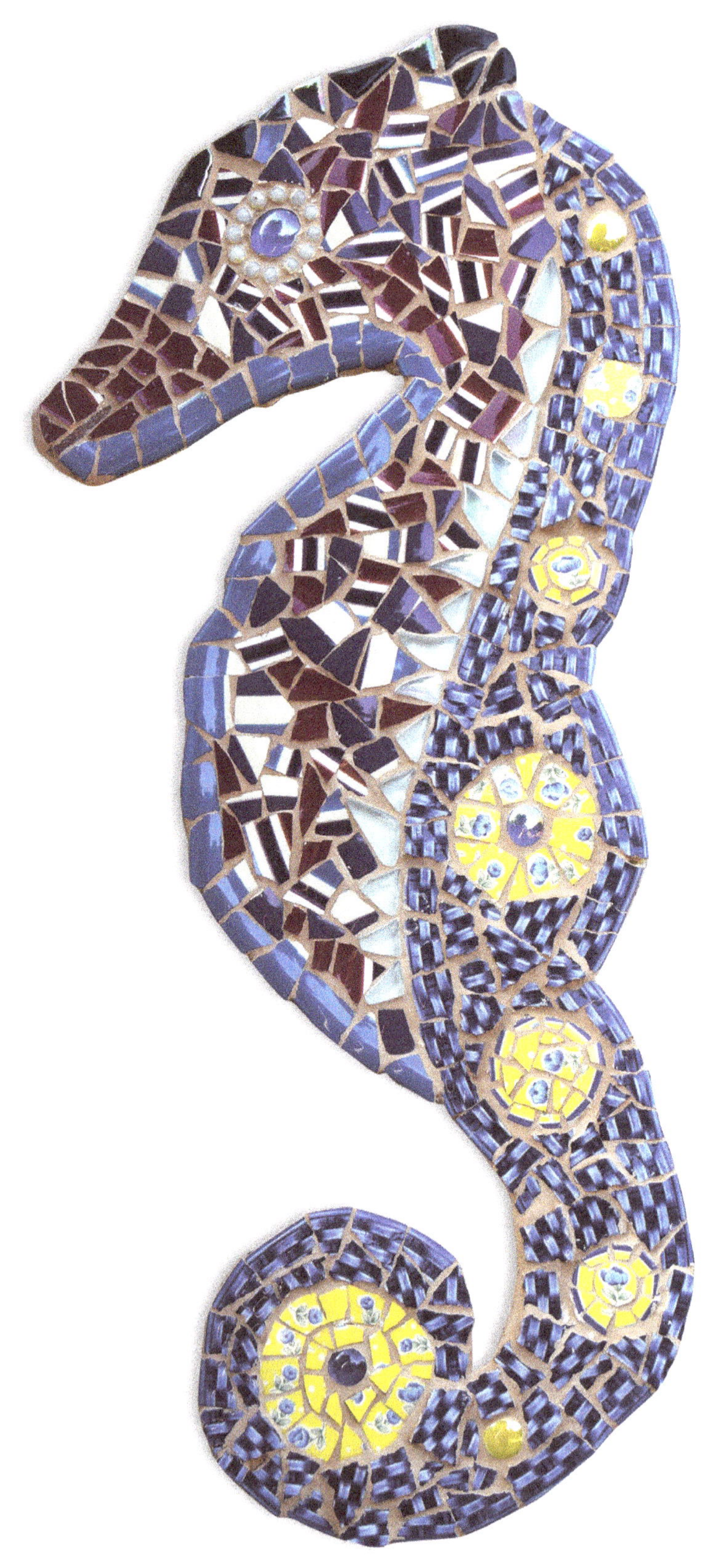

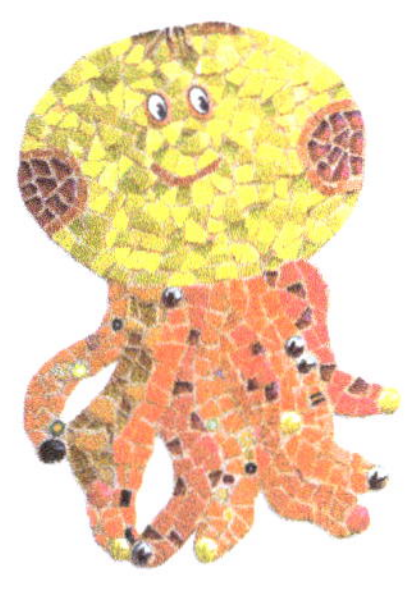

Project: an Octopus

Like the seahorse, this octopus is also made from a combination of several materials - broken plates and cups, polymer clay, round clear glass and even eyes I took from a cup. The main colors are shades of yellow and orange. From there use what you'll find or feel free to change as you need to. The idea here is to recycle unused dishes and combine them into the mosaic piece.

You will need:

Fiberglass mesh cut to the desire size (The original pattern size is 42 cm / 16.4" high)

Clear plastic, a little bit longer than the mesh

Masking tape

Small brush

White glue or carpenter's glue

Outdoor tile adhesive

Trowel

Mosaic Nipper

Plates, cups and mugs – red, yellow and orange shades

Polymer clay flowers or beads

Some round clear glass

Light brown grout

Grout Equipment: mixing bowl, water, a wooden stick, rags, gloves, Small squeegee and dust mask

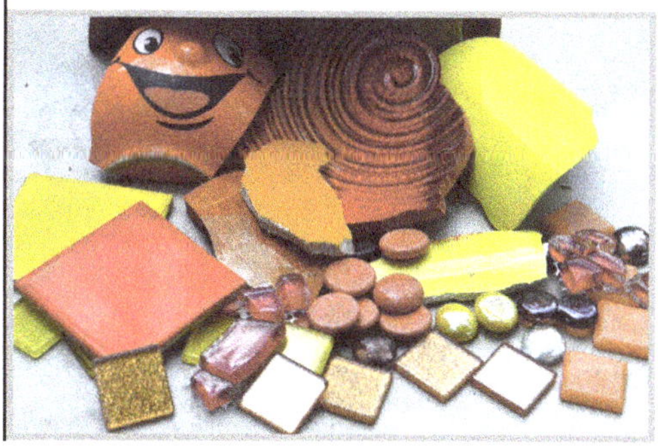

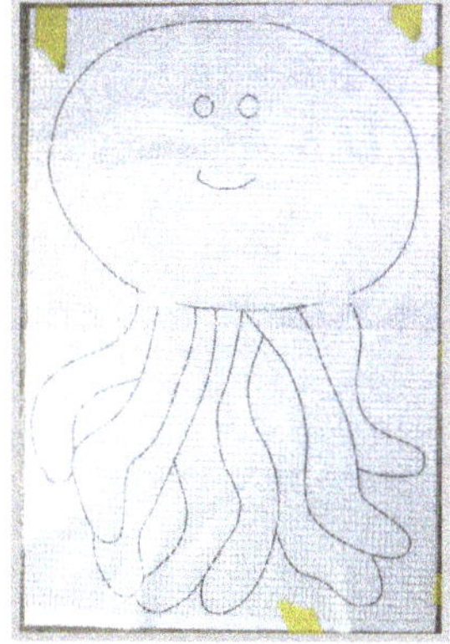

1 Print the octopus pattern in the desired size.

2 Use the masking-tape to paste together the printed paper, plastic and mesh on the working surface.

3 Prepare the mosaic materials: pre-cut all the materials and sort them by shades in separate tools.

5 Cheeks – made from bright red glass and chopped orange contour.

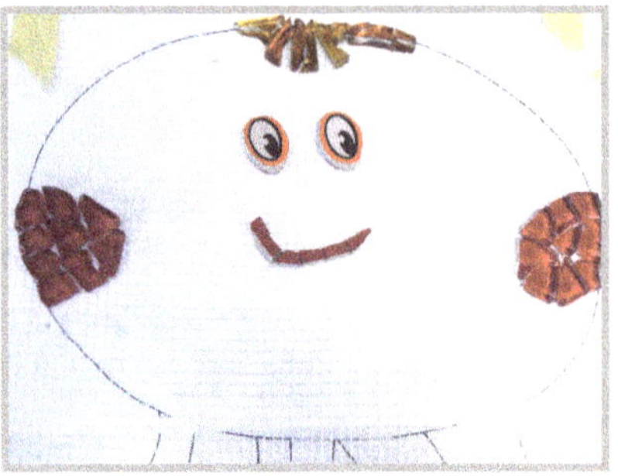

4 Start with the head: pasted eyes with white glue (you can use clear glass circles). Make the mouth from thin strips of red ceramics. Add thin strips of orange or brown for the hair.

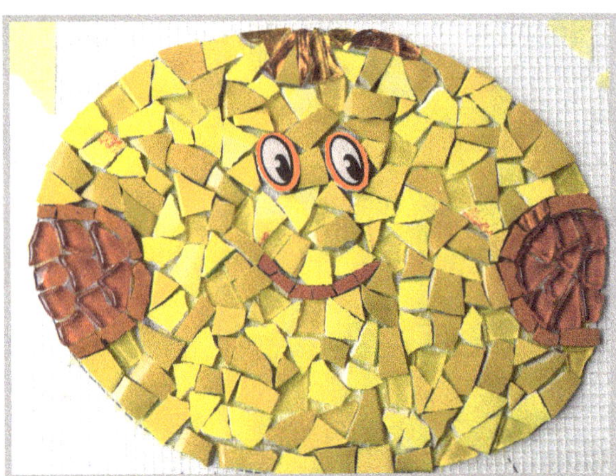

6 Fill the head space with random cut yellow shades of ceramics / cups / plates. Mix multiple shades.

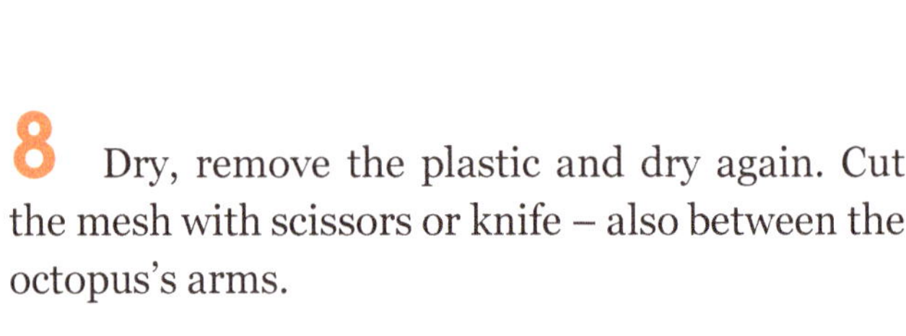

7 The octopus arms: shades of red and orange, each arm in a different color, put clear round glass at the end of each arm. Decorate with polymer clay flowers.

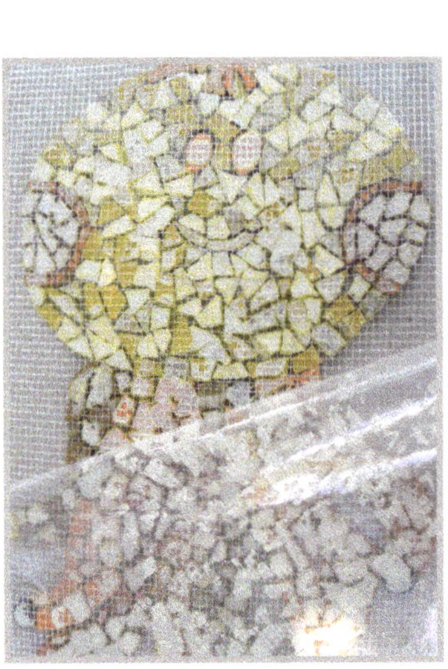

8 Dry, remove the plastic and dry again. Cut the mesh with scissors or knife – also between the octopus's arms.

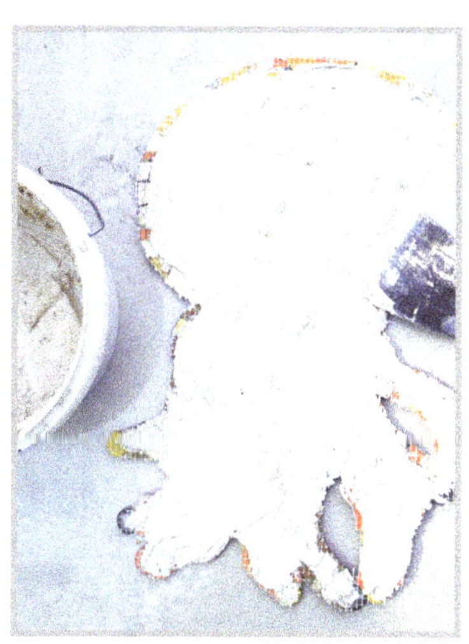

9 repare the paste surface - make sure that the place is clean, smooth slightly if necessary.

10 Applied tile adhesive on the back side of the octopus and push hard to the wall.

11 Compress all the tiles to the wall, this also will strengthen the adhesion and remove the spare glue out.

12 SWith a thin screwdriver remove spare adhesive before everything dries.

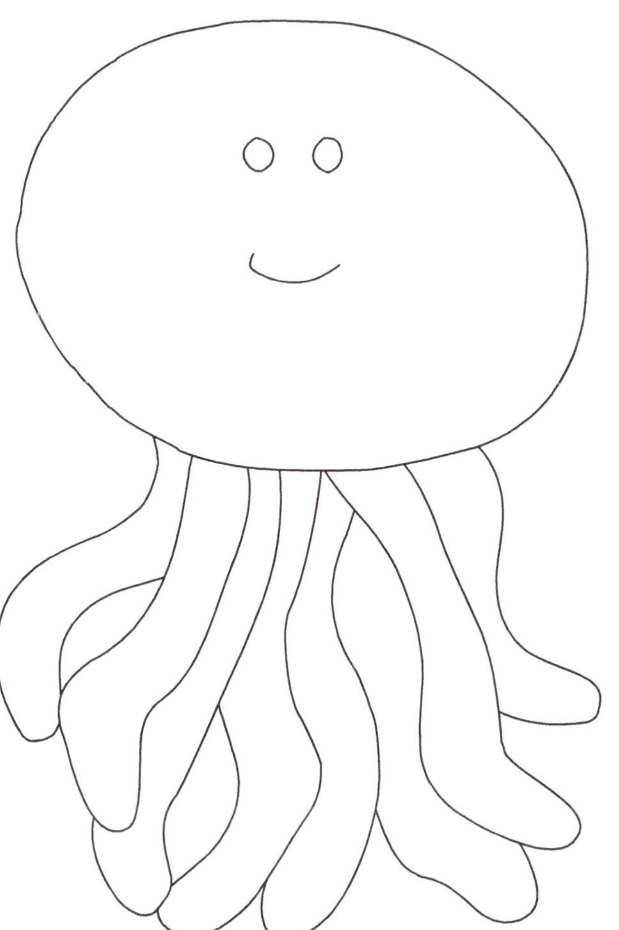

13 Let it dry for at least 24 hours, grout according to grout instructions.

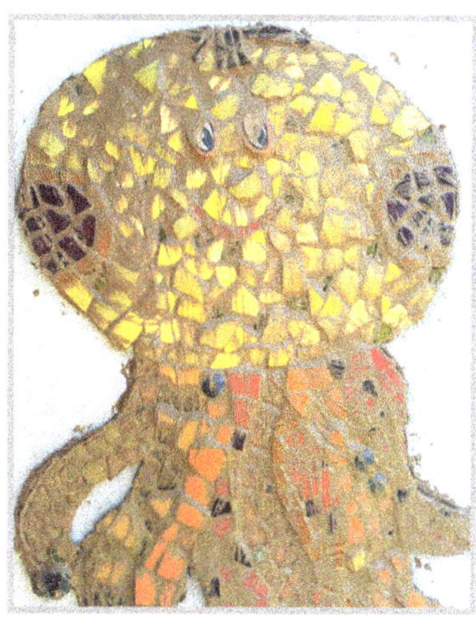

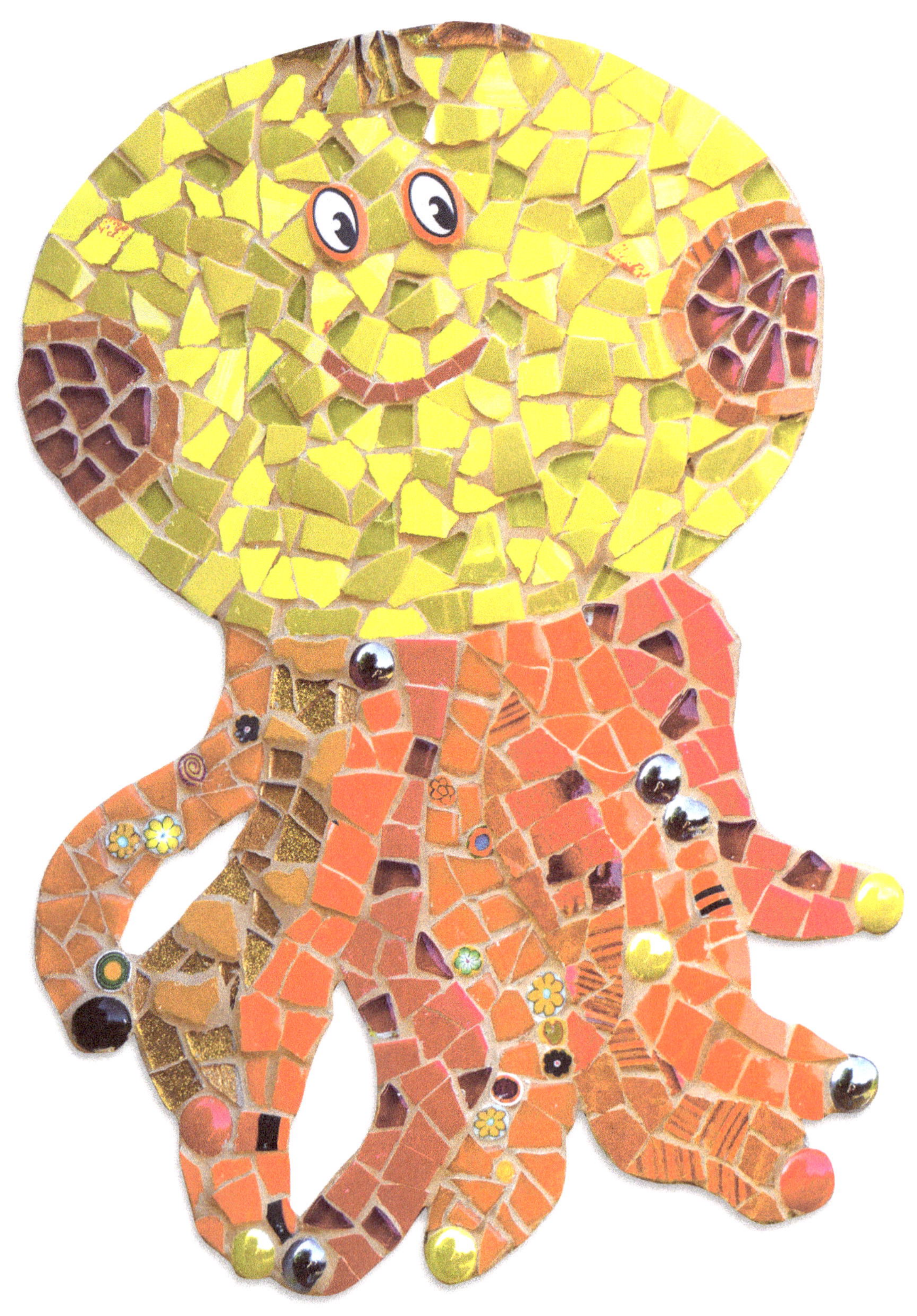

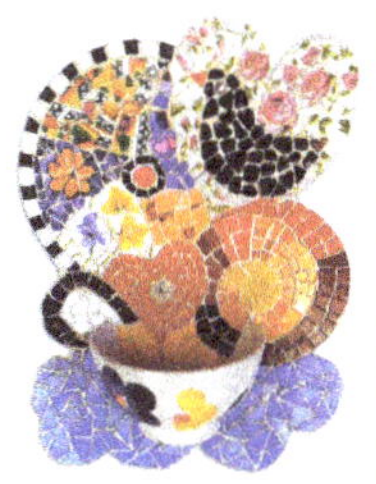

Project: a Happy Bowl

Until now we have broken dishes and used their cut parts in our mosaic art work.

In this project we will use a divided bowl. You can put dried flowers on it, keys or just leave it as is.

Look for a nice ceramic bowl, the kind that serves as a soup or cornflakes bowl. We will crossed it into half and connect into the mosaic work. Now let's add a lot of different materials: fragments of plates and cups, ceramics and more – to make a happy and much more colorful mosaic piece!

In addition, this work combines different kinds of cuts mosaic pieces: triangles, smooth rounded rectangles and random shapes. We will use two types of cutters: mosaic cutter for ceramics cutting and glass nipper for cups and plates cutting.

Tip: It is hard to divide a bowl precisely. Prepare a number of these bowls, cut half and use the best one. This can be done accurately only with an appropriate saw.

You will need:

Fiberglass mesh cut to the desire size (The original pattern size is 38.5 cm / 15" high)

Clear plastic, a little bit longer than the mesh

Masking tape

Small brush

White glue or carpenter's glue

Strong silicone adhesive

Plates, cups and mugs, colorful ceramic, mosaic squares glass

Mosaic nipper

Mosaic cutter

Cream grout

Grout Equipment: mixing bowl, water, a wooden stick, rags, gloves, Small squeegee and dust mask

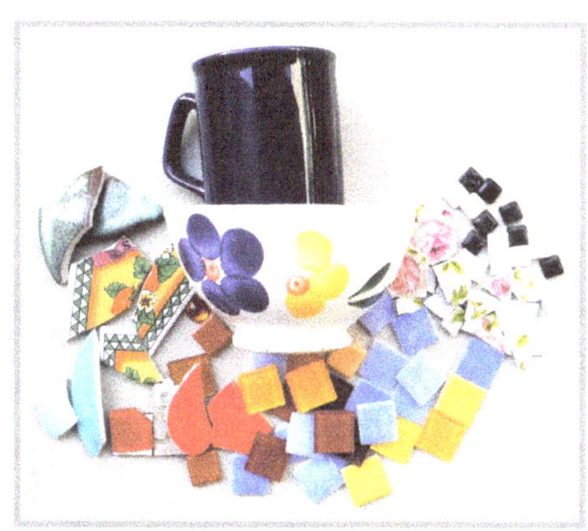

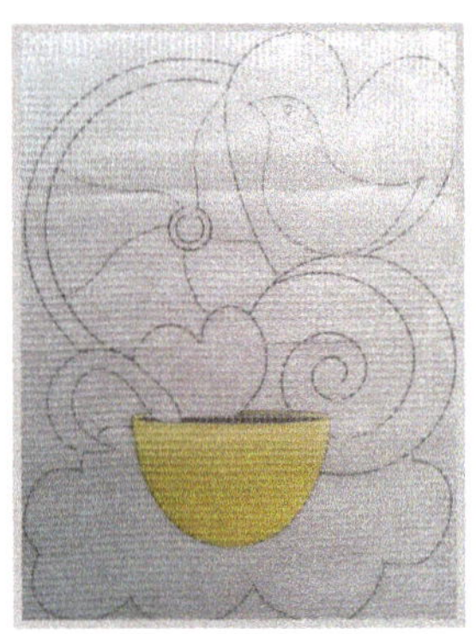

1 Print the pattern in the desired size.

2 Use the masking-tape to paste together the printed paper, plastic and mesh on the working surface.

3 Prepare the mosaic materials: pre-cut all the materials and sort them by shades in separate tools.

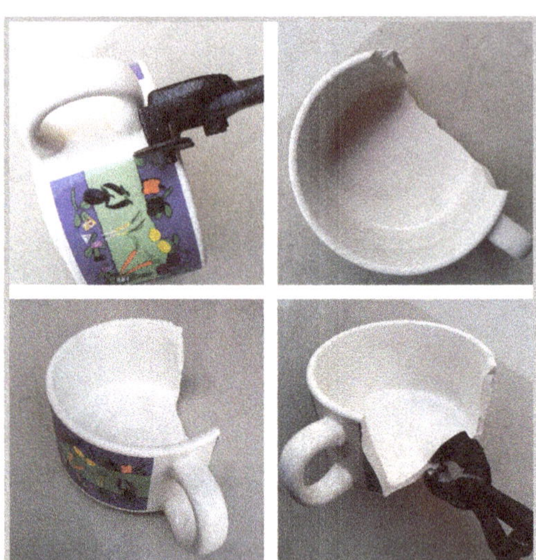

4 The bowl: First divide the bowl into 2 parts: Hold the nipper straight as shown in the picture and cut. Use the mosaic cutter to shape the cut bowl until you have a flat smooth surface. Apply plenty of glue in the area that contact the mesh and press the divided bowl to its place. No matter if there are holes between the bowl and the mesh; we will fill with adhesive when pasted to the final place.

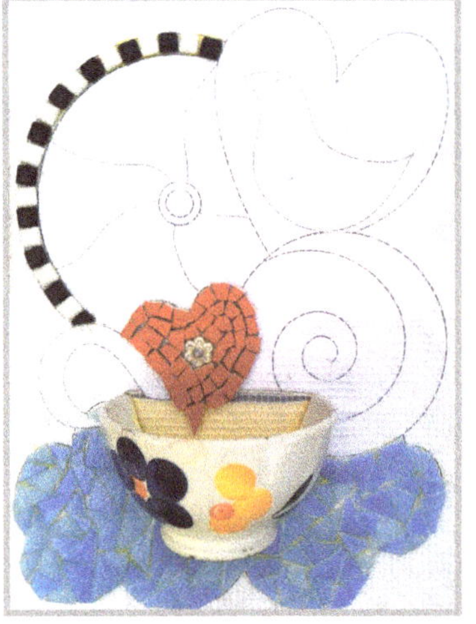

5 Start pasting the mosaic to the mesh: at first - the cloud, made of light blue triangles. It is better to fill with glue a small area at a time and paste the parts on it.

6 Now the heart, made of red cut ceramic tiles. Put a flower in the center (from any kind of found object).

7 The wheel frame is made of small squares of black and white (0.39" / 1 cm).

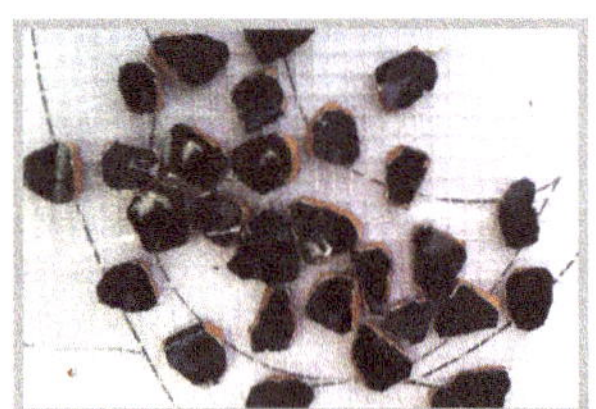

8 The bird has curved parts: cut random shapes from blue ceramic, round the corners of each piece with the mosaic cutter. It may seem to be a hard work but the result is special.

9 Fill the heart behind the bird with cut rose plate.

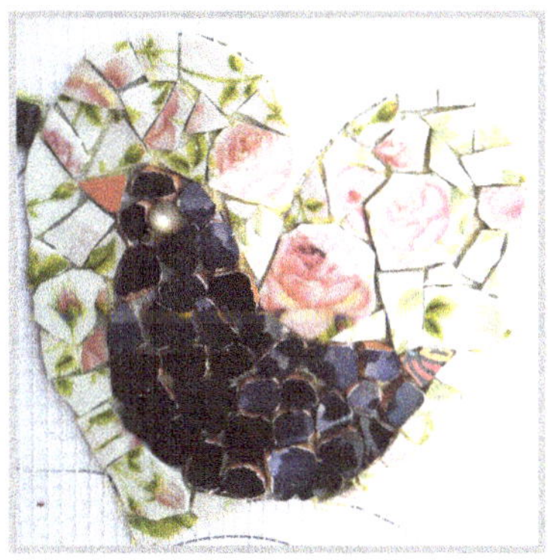

10 The spiral: The spiral is made from cut squares of shiny ceramic tiles and glass, all in shades of yellow - orange - brown. Start from the middle (yellow circle) and move from inside to the outside.

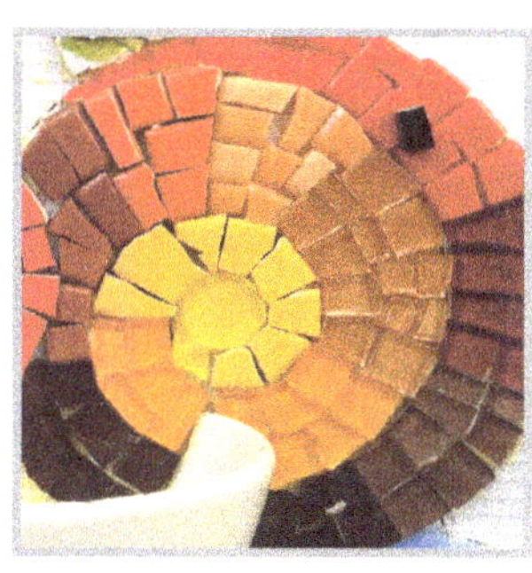

11 Pasted cut ceramic into the bowl (the hidden part) – for complete look.

12 The colored wheel is made of broken cups and plates, each part filled with a different type. The parts shapes are randomly cuts and there are some flowers that where cut from cups and re-glued to the mesh together to keep their original shape.

13 Dry, remove the plastic and dry again. Cut the mesh with scissors or knife.

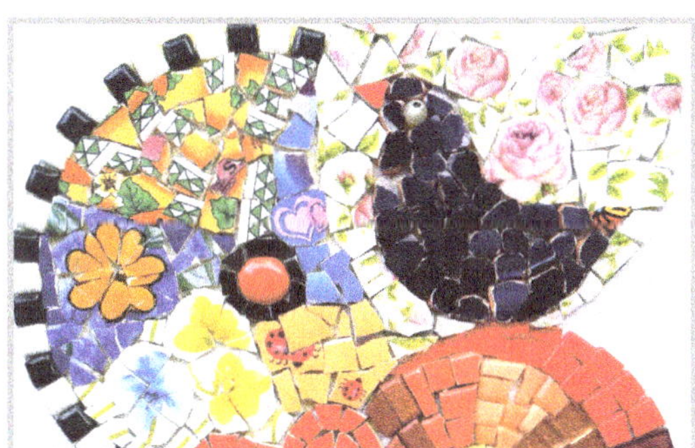

14 Prepare the paste surface - make sure that the place is clean, smooth slightly if necessary.

15 Apply tile adhesive on the back side of the mosaic - it is better to use a strong silicone adhesive, to stable the bowl. Push hard to the wall. It's time to fill the spaces behind the bowl with glue.

Pattern for the bowl:
Enlarge on a photocopier by 410% for a full size design

16 Compress all the tiles to the wall, this also will strengthen the adhesion and remove the spare glue out.

17 With a thin screwdriver remove spare adhesive before everything dries.

18 Let it dry, for at least 24 hours, grout according to grout instructions.

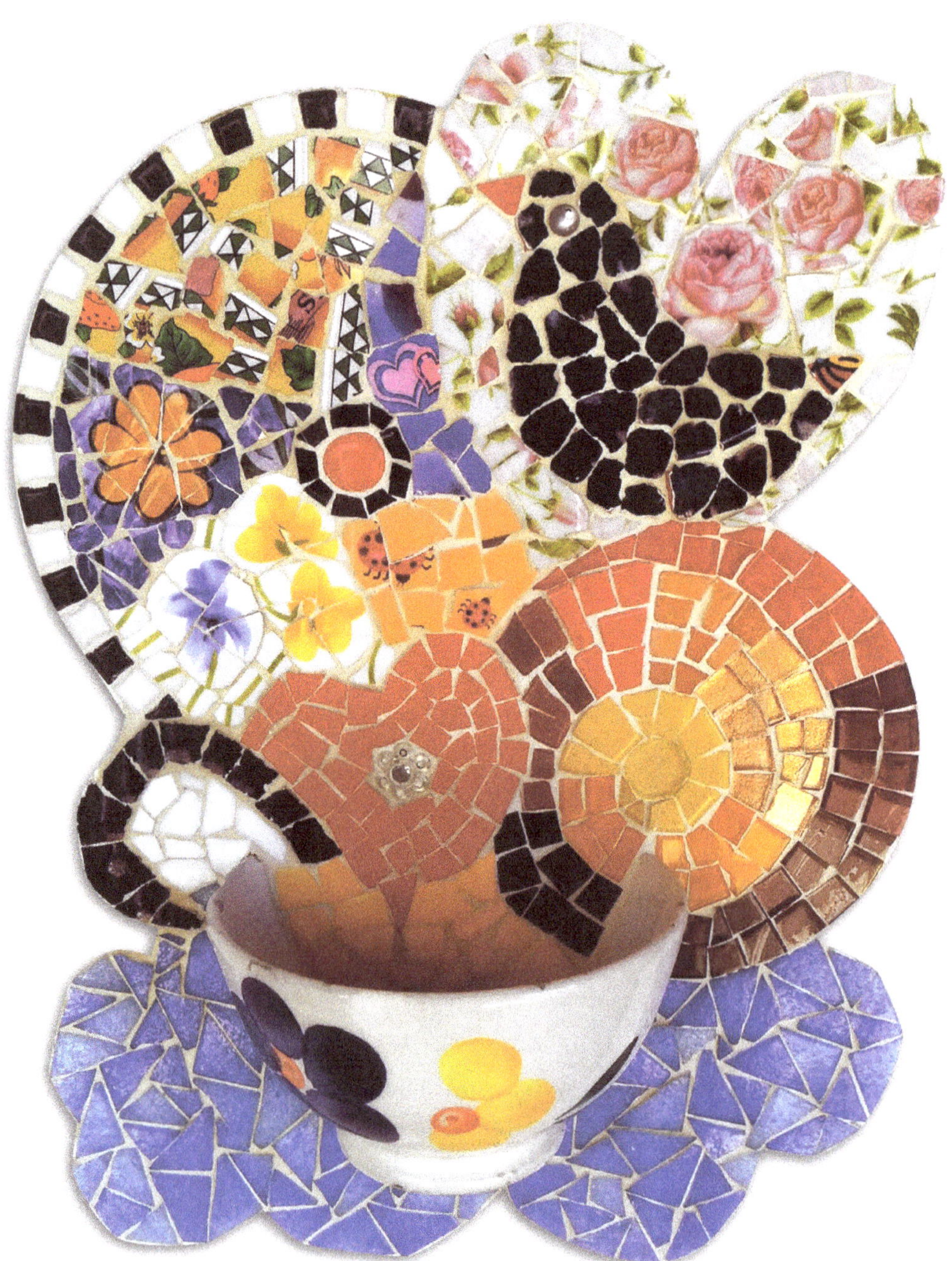

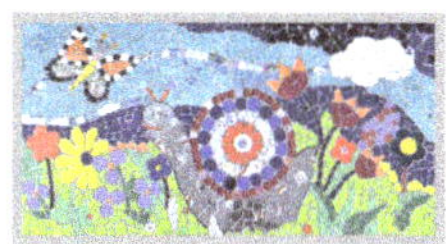

Project: Colorful Floor Rug

The mesh is very suitable for creating floor mats in various sizes. Before working it is necessary to prepare a smooth surface, the best is concrete, which will be the mosaic base. Important note - if the mosaic mat is a walking area, make sure it won't be too smooth to prevent slipping. Colorful bright tiles can make very joyful mosaic work, but smooth floor can be dangerous.

This mosaic rug is a very colorful one. It includes many nature elements - flowers, snail, butterfly and lots of joy. You can increase or decrease according to the required size, and you can paste it on wall instead of floor.

You will need:

Fiberglass mesh cut to the desire size (The original pattern size is 86 cm / 33.9" wide, 42cm / 16.5" high)

Clear plastic, a little bit longer than the mesh

Masking tape

Small brush

White glue or carpenter's glue

Outdoor tile adhesive

Trowel

Mosaic cutter

Colorful ceramic tiles uniform height in different colors (blue, turquoise, light and dark green, gray, yellow, orange, purple, red, brown and white)

Mosaic squares glass – red and shiny gray

Gray grout

Grout Equipment: mixing bowl, water, a wooden stick, rags, gloves, Small squeegee and dust mask

1 Print the rug pattern in the desired size. You can print in parts in your printer and tape together or enlarge in a large printer as one unit.

2 Use the masking-tape to paste together the printed paper, plastic and mesh on the work surface.

3 Prepare the mosaic materials: pre-cut all the materials and sort them by shades in separate tools, especially the light green, turquoise and blue.

4 Start creating the Snail. The snail's "home" is made from circles:

- Put one circle part in the center, it may be with some pattern on it (here with a flower).

- The next 2 rings: ceramic, rectangles shapes with rounded edges, one is red and another with pattern on it.

- The next ring is made of blue ceramic circles.

- In the outer ring put red glass squares.

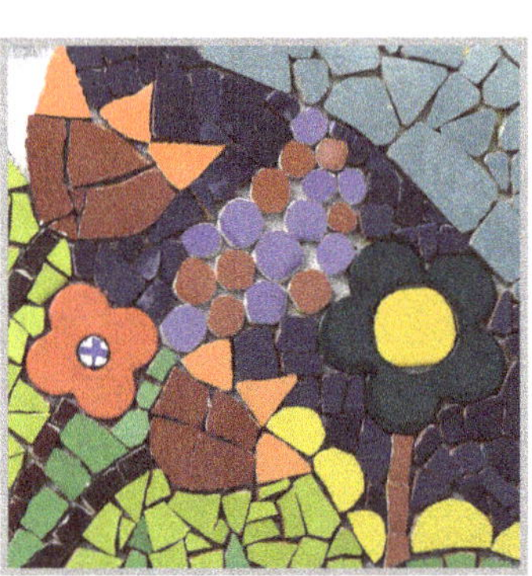

- The snail body is made of gray ceramic parts. Add mouth and 2 antennas from narrow red rectangles, eye and ceramic or polymer clay circle in the antennae end.

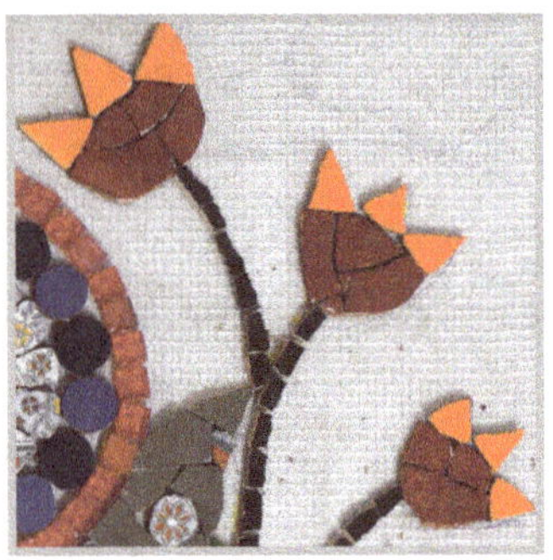

5 Flowers: There is a wide variety of flowers in this floor rug:

- Brown and orange flowers - three orange triangles in each flower and brown ceramics

- Yellow flower - blue circle in the center, yellow rounded petals

- Purple flowers - orange circle at the center, each flower has 3 rounded purple petals

- Some ready flowers - made of cut ceramic flower-shaped. You can replace them with petal-cut flowers as the others we have already made.

- Flower made entirely from two-tone purple circles.

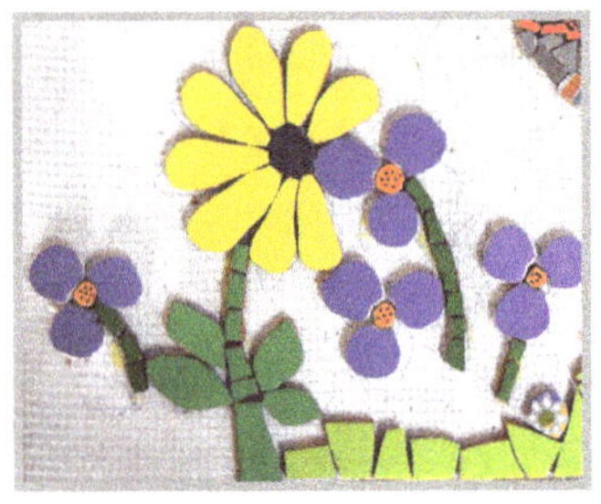

6 Add each flower a stalk, in various shades of green and brown.

7 Grass - made of three shades of green. You can add some little red circles.

8 Butterfly:

- Top pair of wings - frame from black and white ceramic squares, orange fill.

- Lower wings: fill with colorful tiles, add thin black contour.

- Butterfly body made from yellow cut ceramic. Add antennas from gray ceramic and put 2 circles at the end and one for the head. You can use polymer clay for the circles.

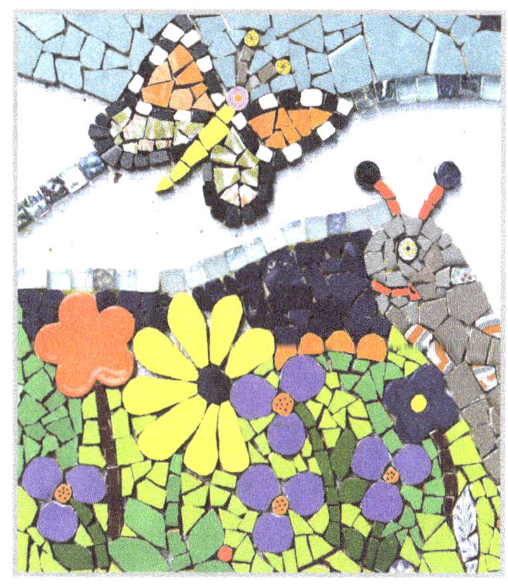

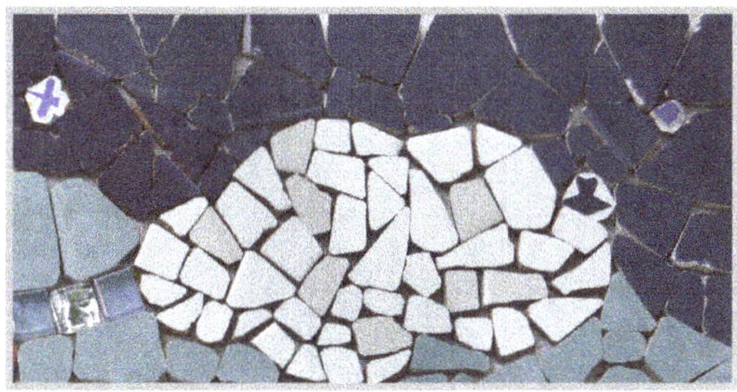

9 The sky: first paste a line made of glossy glass squares, gray and white.

10 Fill the sky areas with cut turquoise and blue ceramics. Please note - all sky parts are rounded edges, to create a different effect.

11 Dry, remove the plastic and dry again. Cut the mesh with scissors or knife.

12 Prepare the rug surface - clean up the pasting place with a brush to remove dust and dirt. Make sure that the place is smooth and straight.

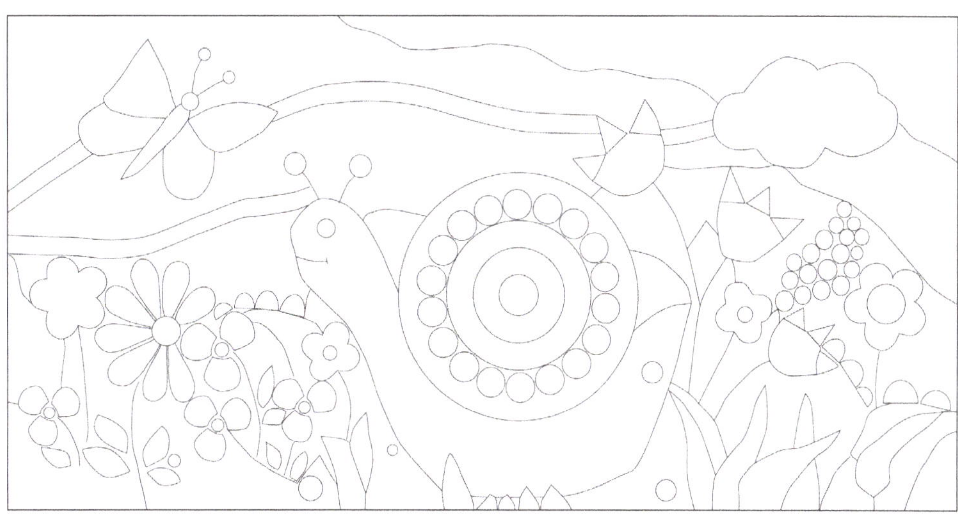

13 Spread tile adhesive evenly on the rugs surface using a trowel. Do not rub too much, otherwise you will work hard cleaning.

14 Take the mosaic rug and paste in place. Press the stones one by one, you can use a straight board for this part. It is important that the rug will be flat as possible.

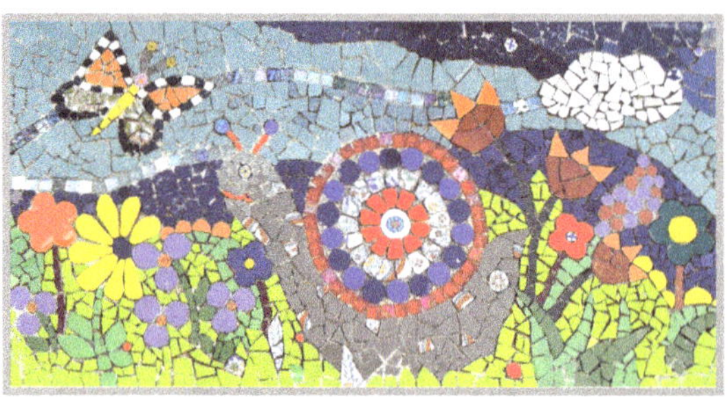

15 With a thin screwdriver remove spare adhesive before everything dries.

16 Let it dry, for at least 24 hours, grout according to grout instruction.

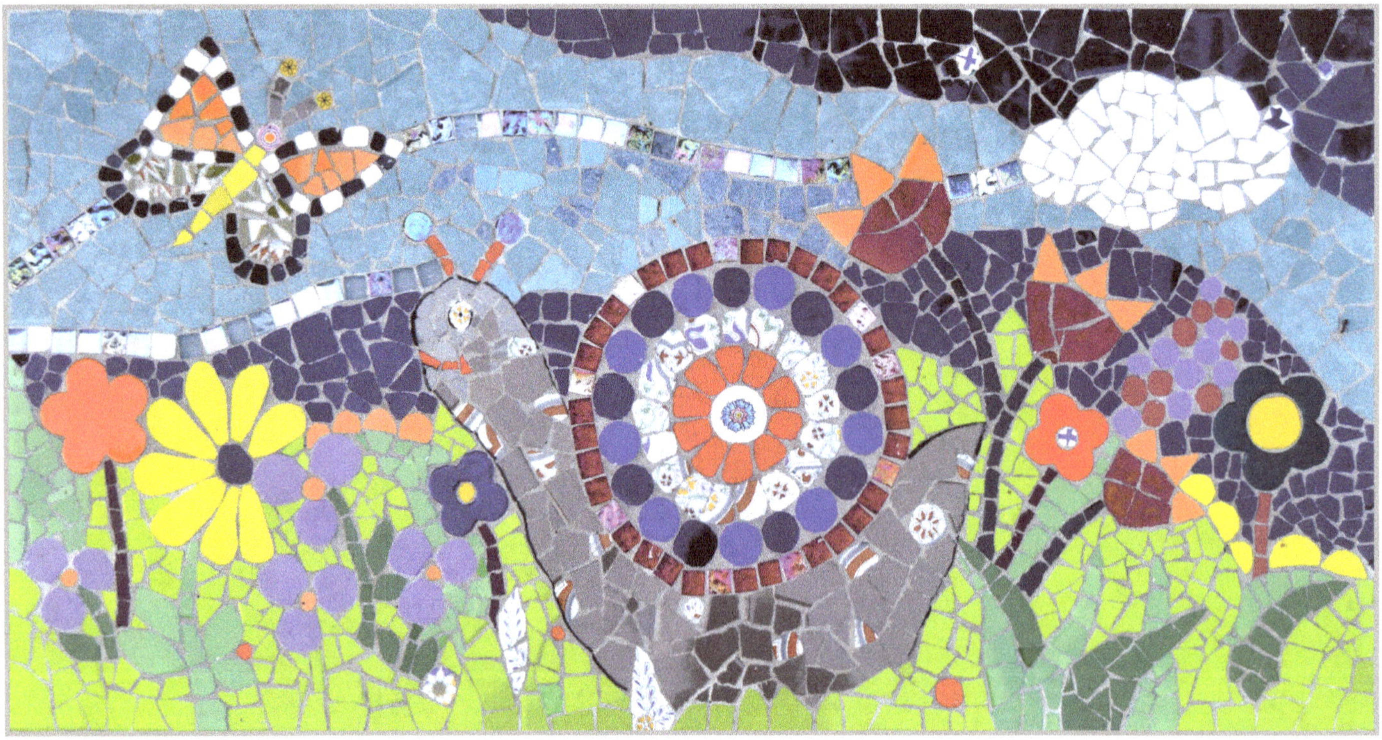

Mosaic Mesh - Pasting on Adhesive Surface

As I said before, we will learn two methods of gluing on mesh.

We talked about the direct adhesion on the mesh and now we will learn how to prepare a surface from mesh and tile adhesive.

In this method, we prepare a base in advance with 2 kind of fiberglass mesh, in different density, covered with layers of tile adhesive. When the surface dries and becomes hard, we glue the mosaic on it, grout and paste the complete unit to the wall.

Benefits:

1. The grout process is made on our working table, horizontally, not on the wall in inconvenient conditions. This is the main advantage of this method.

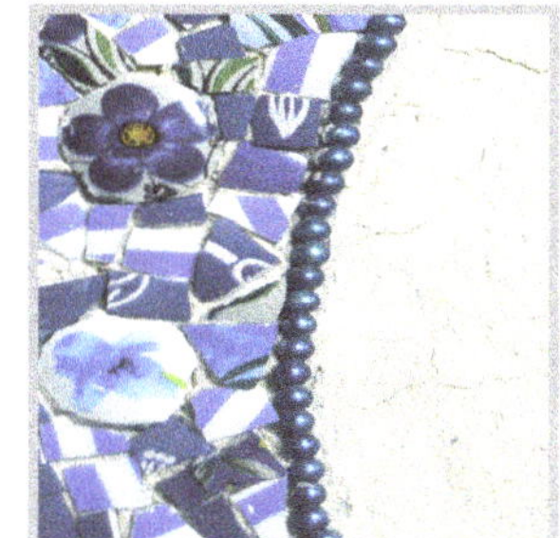

2. Easy pasting on the wall: just spread the appropriate glue behind the piece, compress it to the place and that's it!

3. It is possible to create inside the mosaic piece curved elements or three - dimensional (like rounded body for a butterfly or beetle).

Disadvantages:

1. It is difficult to copy complex samples to the surface.

2. You should pay attention not to create delicately thin shapes that may break during you work.

3. Longer work process, consists of several stages and requires waiting between steps.

4. The mosaic glue in this method is tiles adhesive that needs to be cleaned from time to time in the workflow.

Working method:

1. Print the desired mosaic pattern in the appropriate size and cut around the paper.

2. Prepare the base: measure the size you need and prepare the surface slightly larger.

3. Spread out on the table the clear plastic. Put on it 2 kind of fiberglass mesh, cut to the desired size: first the wide-holes mesh and on the top the tense one. Tape it all together with masking tape to your working base to prevent displacement. You can put either 2 layers of the same mesh; just rotate the top mesh slightly to tighten the surface.

4. Using a trowel spread the first layer of tile adhesive on the mesh surface. It is important that the first layer will be thin and uniform. If it will be too thick, it will be hard to cut.

5. Dry and wait for the surface will be hard - drying time is varies, depending on the weather conditions, at least half an hour.

6. When the surface is hard enough, copy the pattern contour on it: take the cut out paper, lay it on the adhesive base and mark around with a pencil.

7. Cut the base with the plastic underneath with a knife or scissors.

8. Make another layer on the cut base: put some newspapers or clear plastic below the base. Using a trowel applied another layer of tile adhesive. Again it is important to keep a straight and smooth layer as possible, because this will be the final working base. Align and smooth all the edges. If you want to raise some parts of your mosaic work, this is the time to do it. Take some tile adhesive with a spatula or a wood stick and design the shape.

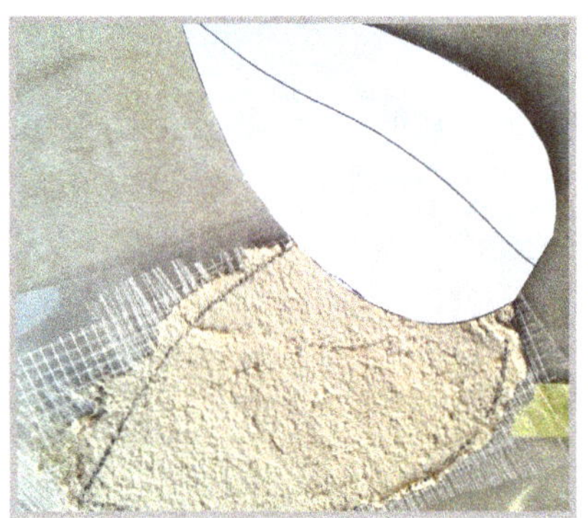

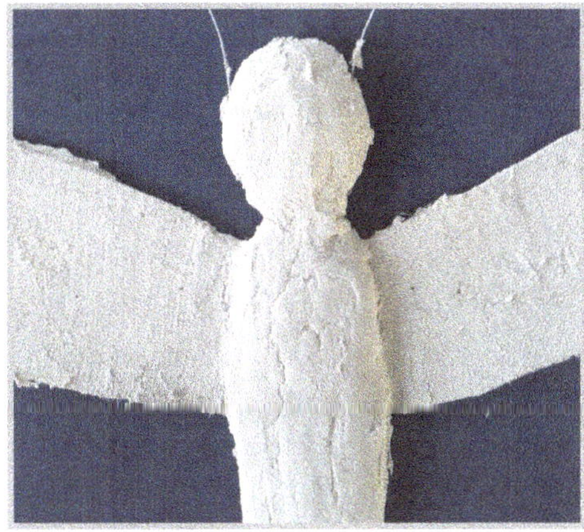 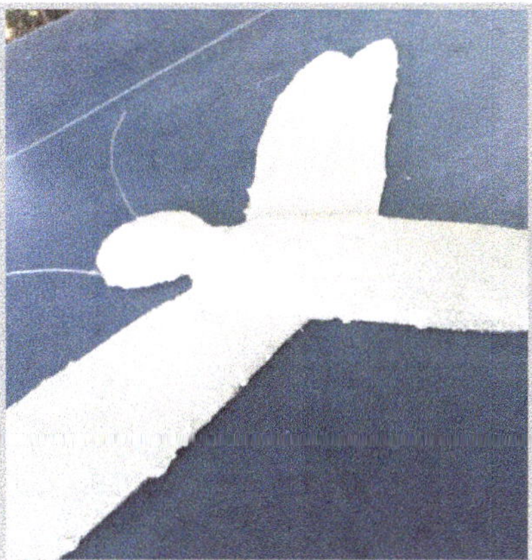

9. Dry again, until you get a dry and hard surface.

10. If you have more details in your pattern you want to copy to the surface, do the following steps:

    - Flip the paper with the printed sample to the other side.

    - Paint the outline of the drawing with dark Panda color. This color will serve as a copy paper.

    - Flip the painted paper, put it on the prepared base, the panda color is facing the base.

    - With a pencil go over all the contours until you copy the entire design.

    - Go over the lines with a pencil if necessary.

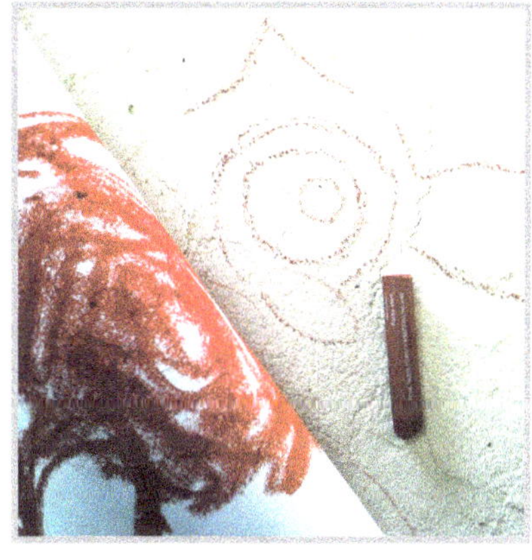

11. The base is ready! Paste the mosaic on it with tile adhesive.

12. Wait at least 24 hours and grout – see grout instructions.

13. Pasting on the wall: remove the plastic. On the back side of your mosaic work spread strong acrylic mastic. Always follow the manufacturer's directions. Hold and push the piece to the place until it stuck. Note that the work is not sliding down while installing.

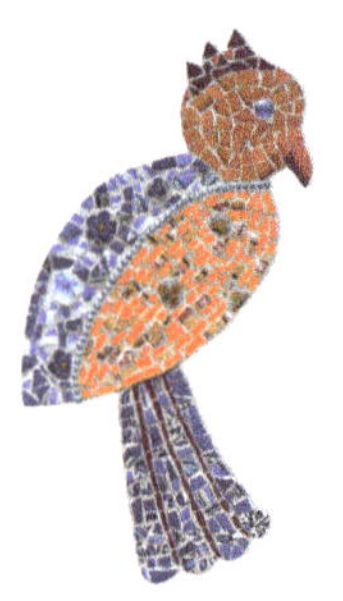

Project: an Orange Bird on Ready Mesh Base

This bird is made of two separate parts, which will gather together on the wall. The reason for the separation is purely practical - utilization of surface space we have created. Use colored cups and plates for different textures.

You will need:

Wide Fiberglass mesh cut to the desire size (The original pattern size is 40 cm / 15.6" high)

Thin Fiberglass mesh cut to the desire size

Clear plastic, a little bit longer than the mesh

Masking tape

Wooden stick

Tile adhesive

Strong silicone adhesive

Trowel

Pencil

Mosaic cutter

Wheeled glass nipper

A long bead chain

Ceramic plates and cups, orange and blue shades

One blue round clear glass

Cream grout

Grout Equipment: mixing bowl, water, a wooden stick, rags, gloves, Small squeegee and dust mask

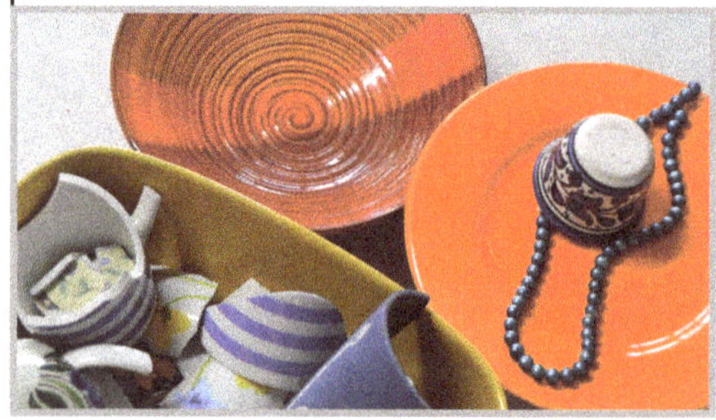

1 Print the bird pattern in the desired size and cut.

2 Prepare one layer of mesh base according to the instructions.

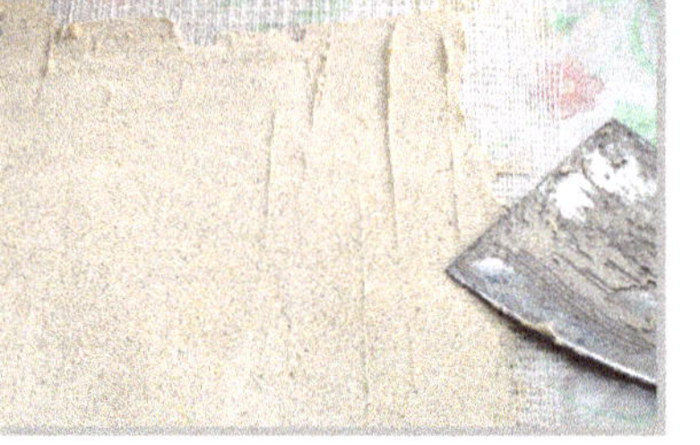

3 Copy the design of the bird to the base in two parts - the body and the head in one unit, the tail as a separate unit and cut.

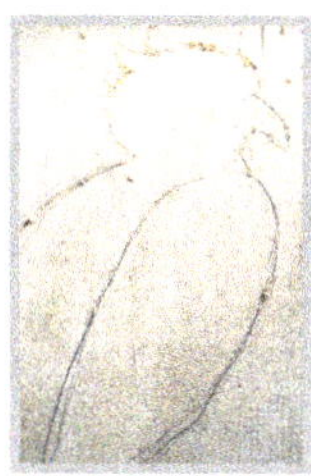

4 Spread another smooth layer of tile adhesive, using the trowel, and let dry.

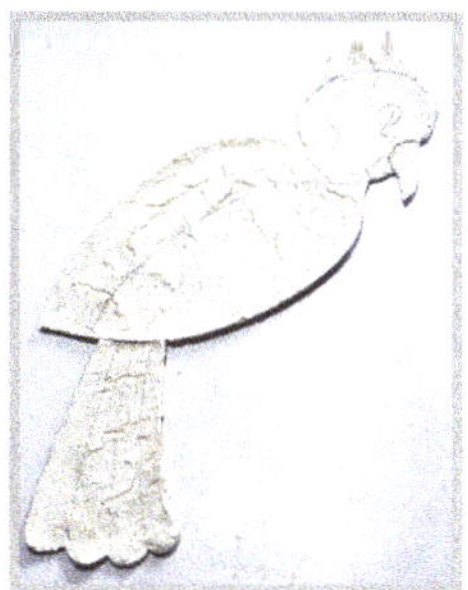

5 Using a pencil mark the eye, head, wing, and length lines in the tail.

6 Prepare all mosaic materials: pre-cut all the materials and sort by separate colors. Cut cups and plates with the mosaic nipper.

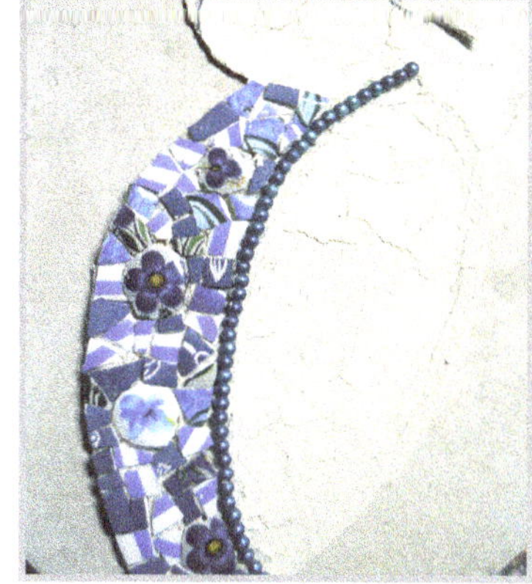

7 Start with the body: stick the chain that separating the body and wing.

8 The bird's body is made of broken cups and plates in blue shades.

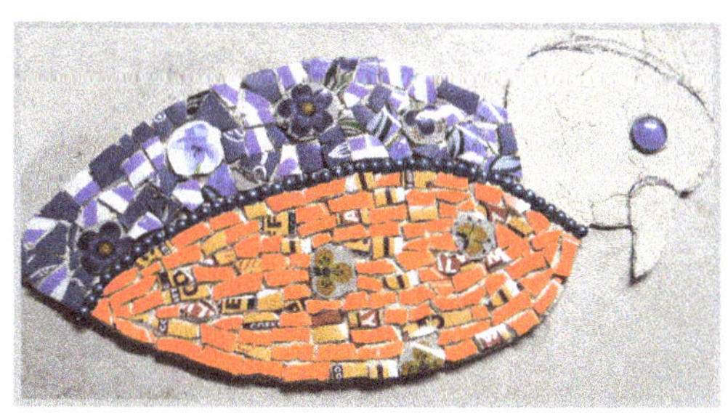

9 The Wing is made of orange broken plates and cups, cut into narrow rectangles. You can add some cut flowers. Stick them together toward the wing in the same direction.

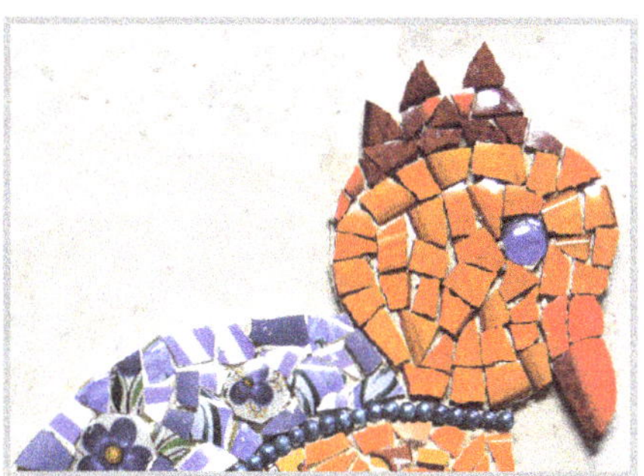

10 Put a blue round clear glass for the eye and a beak - cut as one piece.

11 The head is made of broken orange cups, emphasize the tassel with darker color.

12   Tail: First Cut brown ceramic into thin strips and paste three separation lines.

13   Fill the rest in blue parts of plates and cups cut into small pieces.

14   Keep your work clean from adhesive residue.

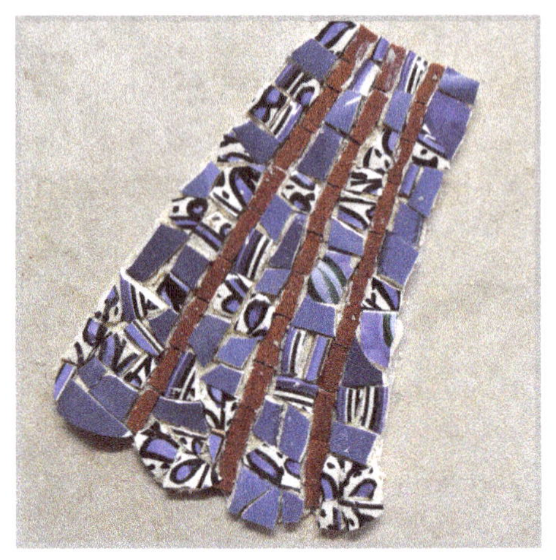

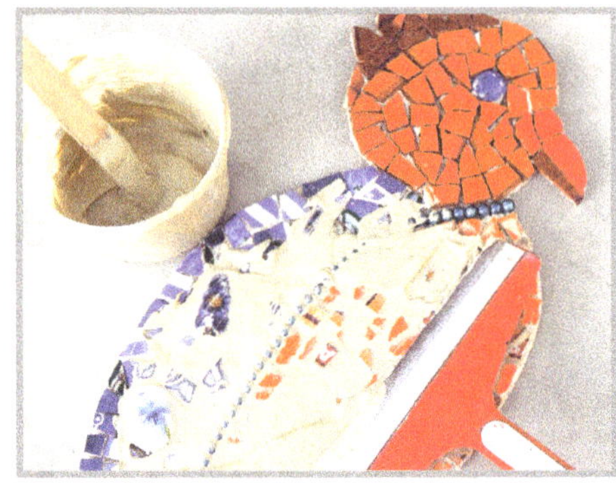

15   Wait at least 24 hours and grout – see grout instructions.

16   Remove the plastic and spread strong acrylic mastic on each part of the bird's back. Hold and push the piece to the place until it stuck – First the body, then set the tile in place.

> **Pattern for the Bird:**
> Enlarge on a photocopier by 290% for a full size design

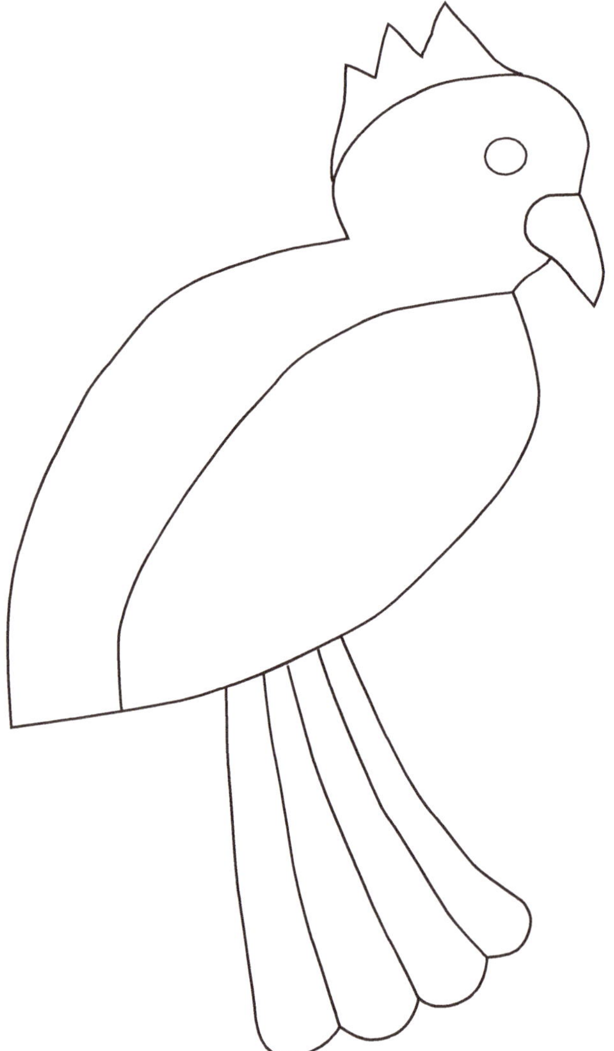

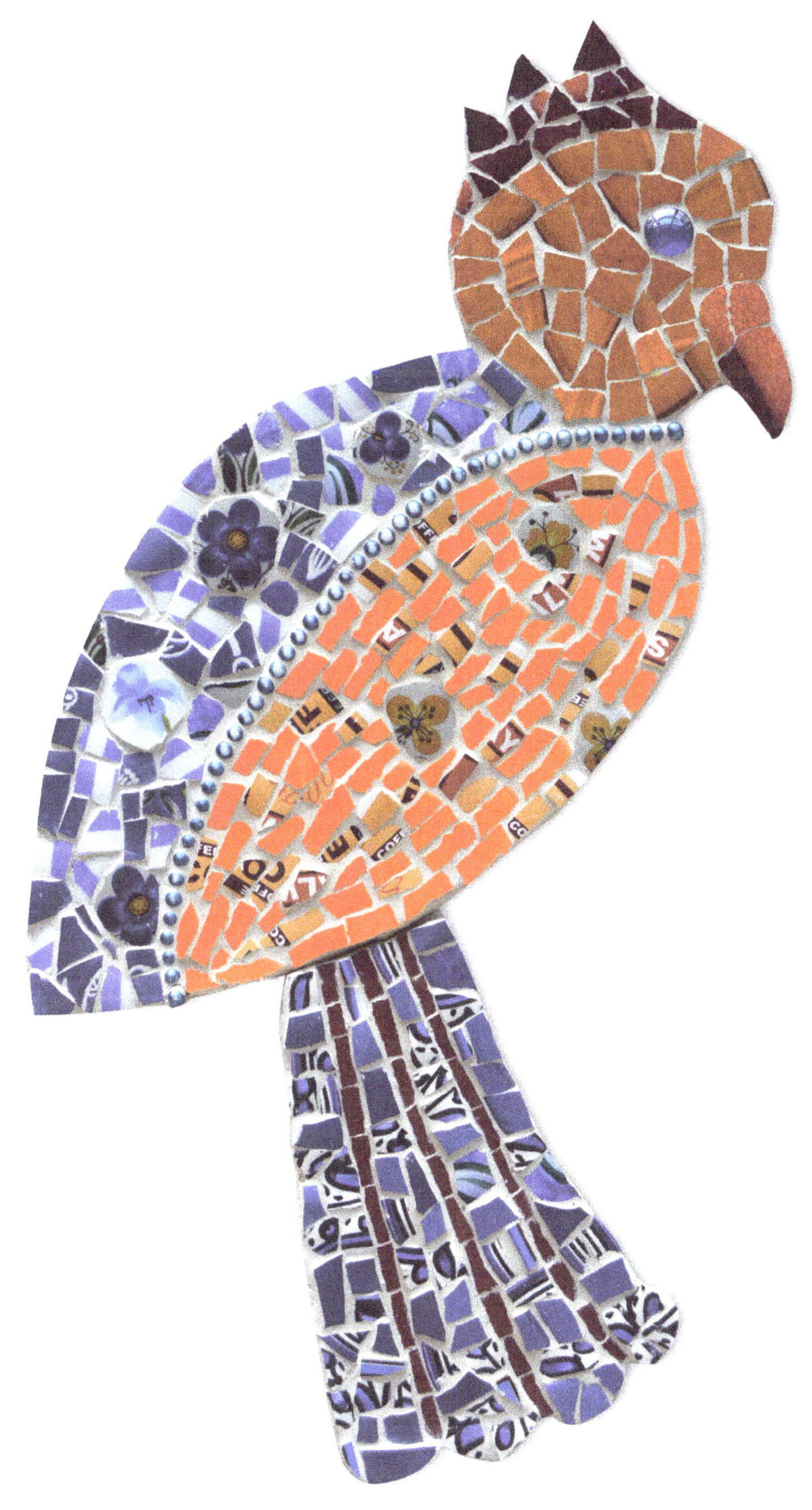

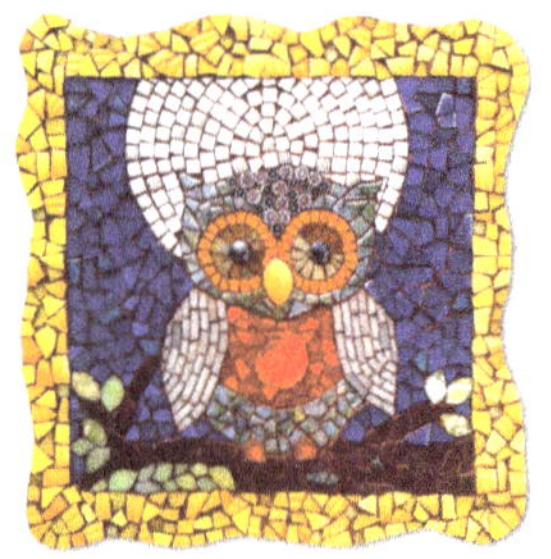

Project: An Owl In Moonlight On Ready Mesh Base

I have noticed that people have a special affection for owls. This is an animal that symbolizes the wisdom and has big and watching eyes.

This owl has a bright yellow frame that emphasizes it and made of different materials. You can take this as an inspiration. You are welcome to modify and integrate any materials or colors that are right for you, in this mosaic work.

You will need:

Wide Fiberglass mesh cut to the desire size (The original pattern size is 44 cm / 17" high)

Thin Fiberglass mesh cut to the desire size

Clear plastic, a little bit longer than the mesh

Masking tape

Wooden stick

Tile adhesive

Strong silicone adhesive

Trowel

Pencil

Mosaic cutter

Wheeled glass nipper

Ceramic plates and cups, orange and blue shades

White and gray mosaic small Squares

One blue round clear glass

Broken cups and plates with cut ceramic tiles in shades of yellow, blue, red, brown

Green and blue glass mosaic tiles

Glass in shades of orange and brown

2 round clear glass

Polymer clay flowers

Brown grout

Grout Equipment: mixing bowl, water, a wooden stick, rags, gloves, Small squeegee and dust mask

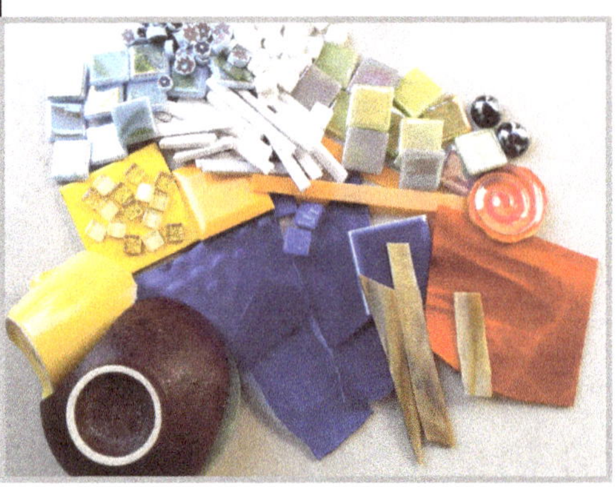

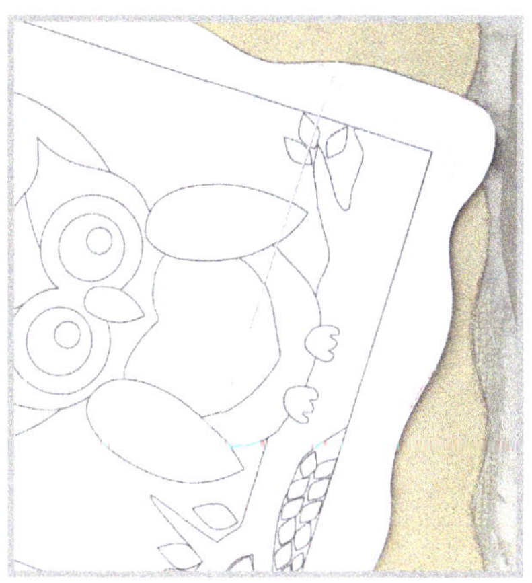

1 Print the owl pattern in the desired size and cut.

2 Prepare one layer of mesh base according to the instructions.

3 Copy the owl's frame to the prepared base and cut.

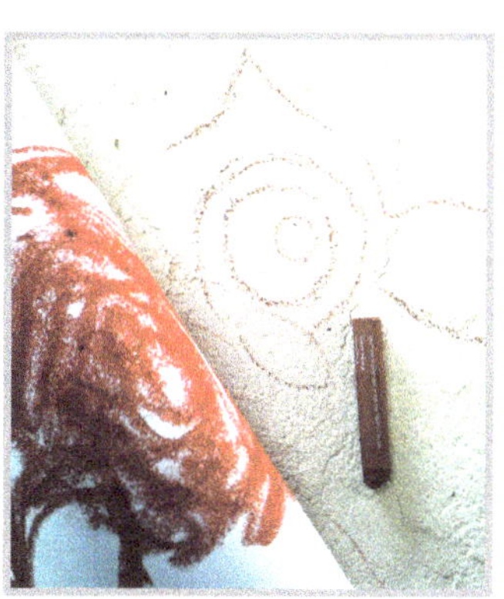

4 Spread one more smooth layer of tile adhesive using the trowel and let dry.

5 Copy the owl design to the base. Use the Panda color method (see instructions before).

6 Prepare all mosaic materials: pre-cut all the materials and sort by separate colors. Cut cups and plates with the mosaic nipper.

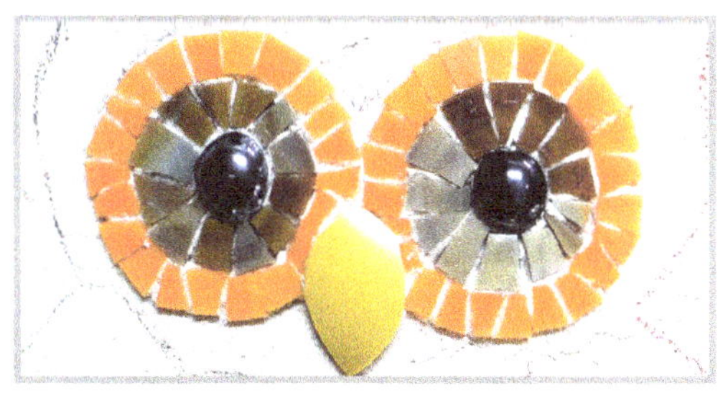

7 Start with the owl's head: butter the round clear glass with tile adhesive and put in the center of the eye. Circle it with brown glass parts and another circle of orange glass. Center a big yellow beak cut in a leaf shape (you can cut it from glass, to get a round beak as pictured).

8 In the triangle above the eyes pasted polymer clay flowers or other round parts.

9 Fill the rest of the head with cut light blue glass squares.

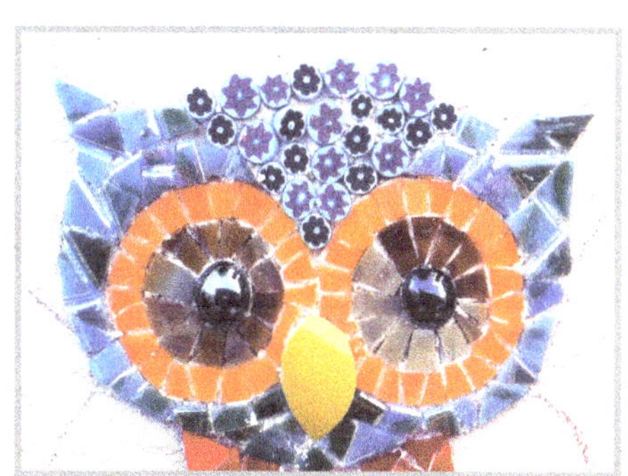

10   The belly is filled with red cut plates. The spiral at the center was taken from the bottom of a ceramic bowl.

11   Fill the wings with white ceramic strips. Begin with the long inner band and move outward.

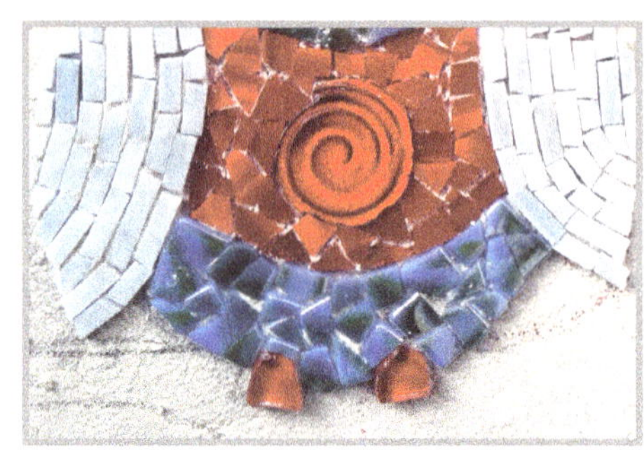

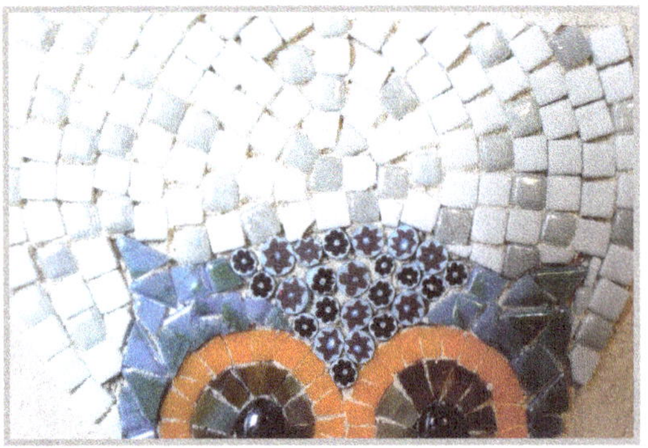

12   Use the same glass squares you use for the head to fill the bottom of the owl. Add red legs.

13   The moon over the owl's head: stick white and gray shades in circles from outside to inward.

14   dd brown branch and leafs from green glass squares.

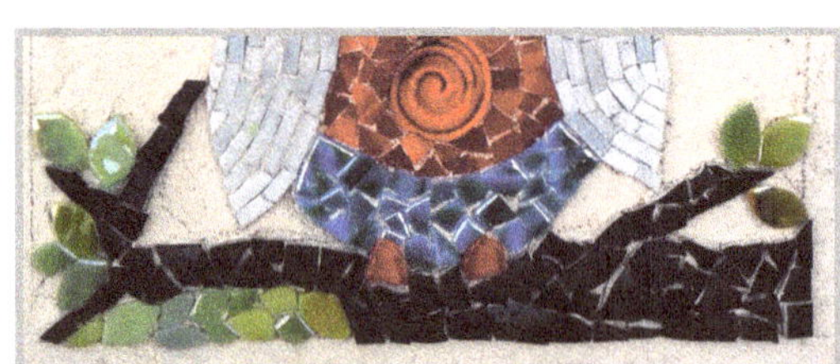

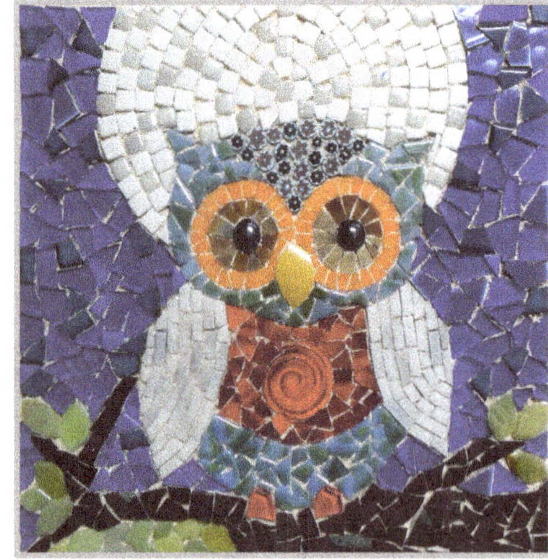

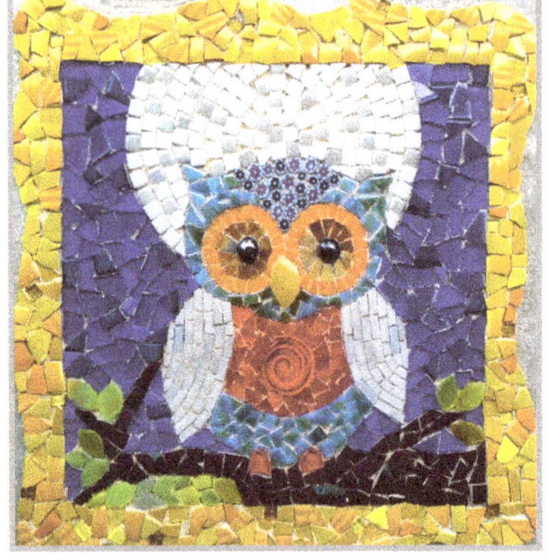

15   Fill the background in blue shades - mix of ceramic, cups and plates, depending on the desired shades.

16   Add a yellow frame - a blend of gold and yellow shades. Choose tile or plates as you want.

17   Keep your work clean from adhesive residue.

18   Wait at least 24 hours and grout – see grout instructions.

19   Remove the plastic and spread strong acrylic mastic on the owl's back side. Hold until it is stuck in place.

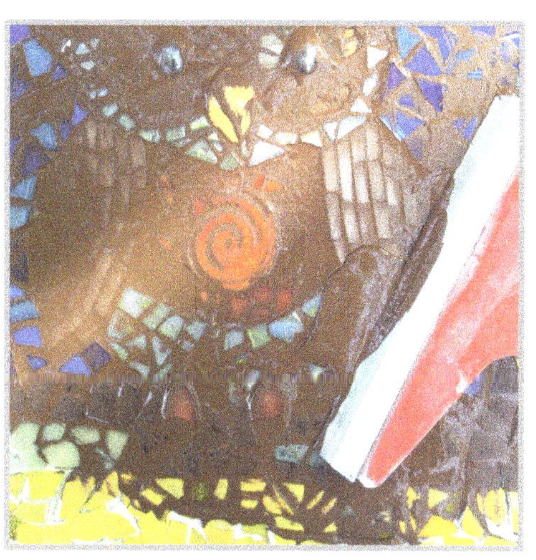

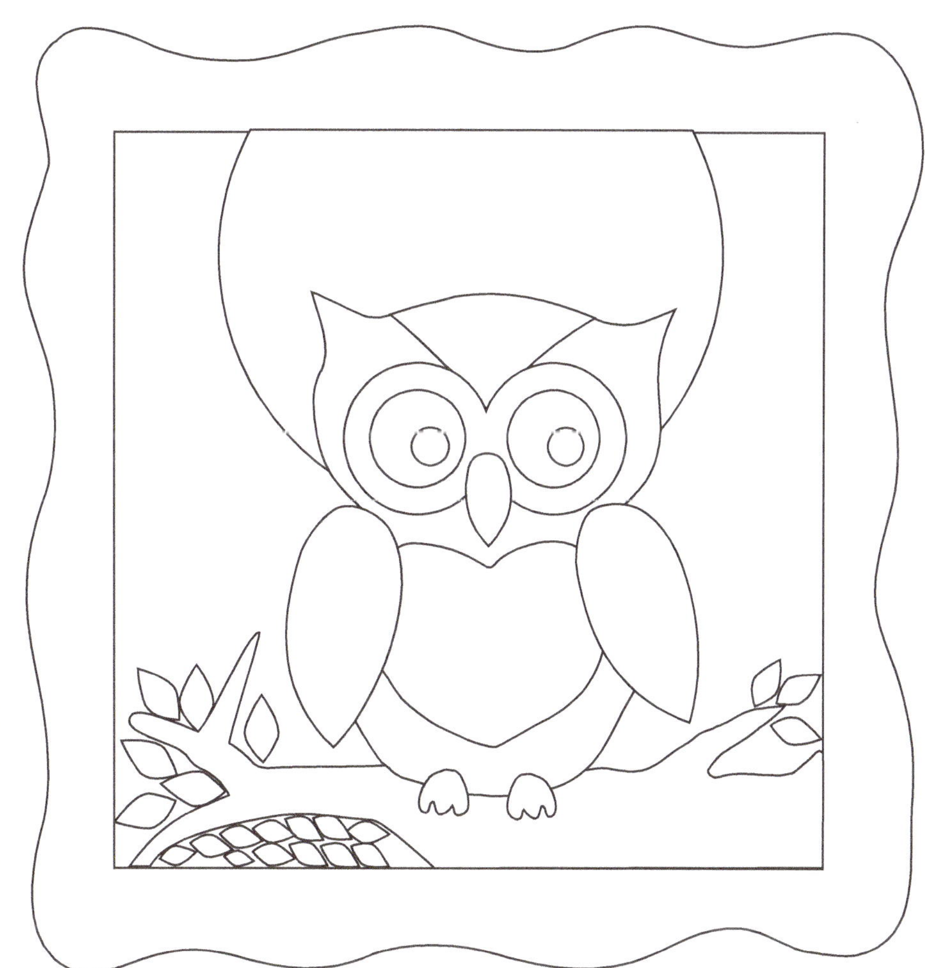

Pattern for the Owl:
Enlarge on a photocopier by 350% for a full size design

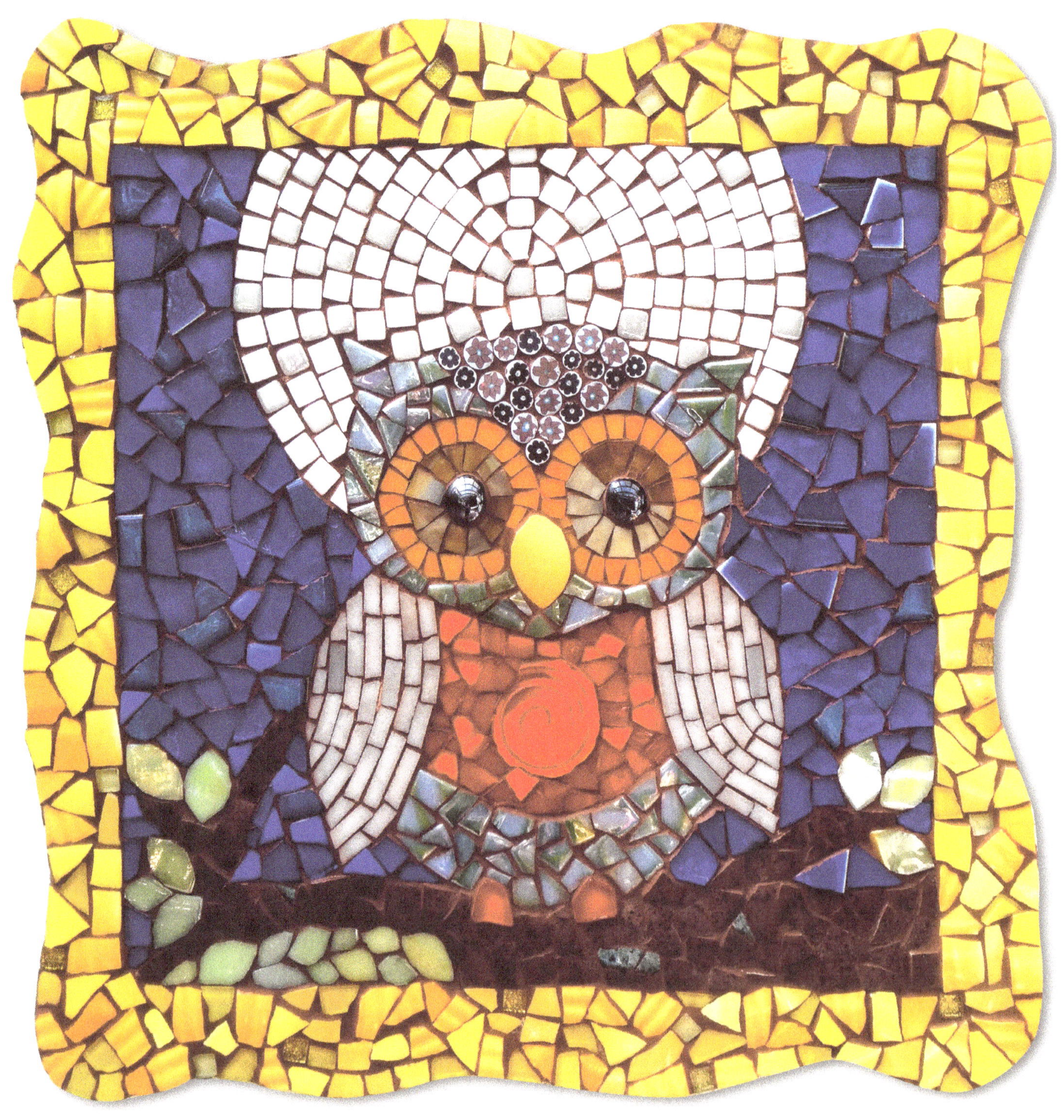

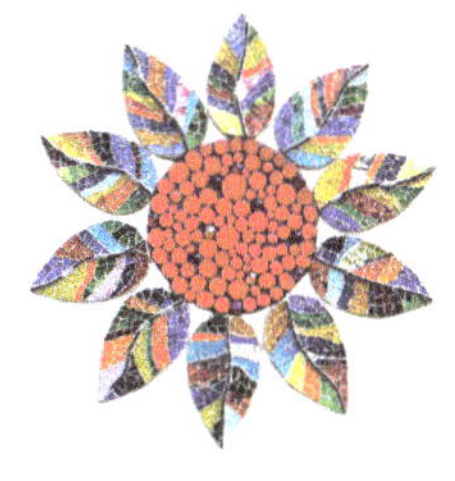

PROJECT: A GIANT FLOWER ON READY MESH BASE

This flower is built from separate parts of the central circle and leaves. You can create it in any size or color you want and it will be a great decoration to any wall, outside or inside. The flower is made of two types of materials: ceramics tiles in the center and glass in various colors for the leaves. It is a great way to use leftover pieces of colored glass. In addition you can choose any color you want for the leaves and do this flower in shades of one color.

You will need:

Wide Fiberglass mesh cut to the desire size (The original pattern size is 64 cm / 43.2" high)

Thin Fiberglass mesh cut to the desire size

Clear plastic, a little bit longer than the mesh

Masking tape

Wooden stick

Tile adhesive

Strong silicone adhesive

Trowel

Pencil

Mosaic cutter

Wheeled glass nipper

Red ceramic tiles

Red round clear glass

Colorful stained glass

Cream and black grout

Grout Equipment: mixing bowl, water, a wooden stick, rags, gloves, Small squeegee and dust mask

1   Print the circle of the flower's center and one leaf in the desired size and cut.

2   Prepare one layer of mesh base according to the instructions.

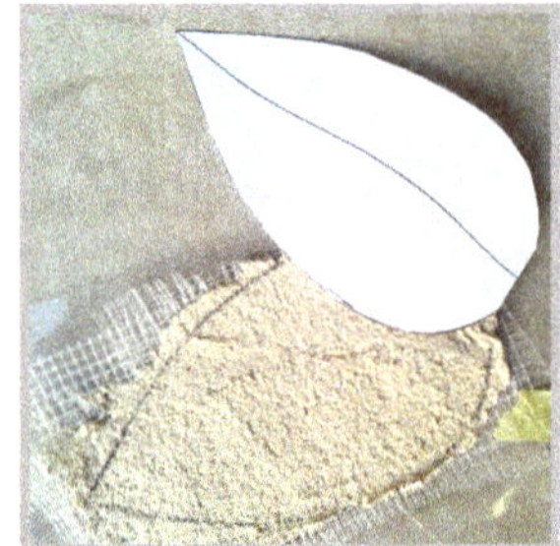

3   Copy the circle and 10 leaves to the mesh base and cut.

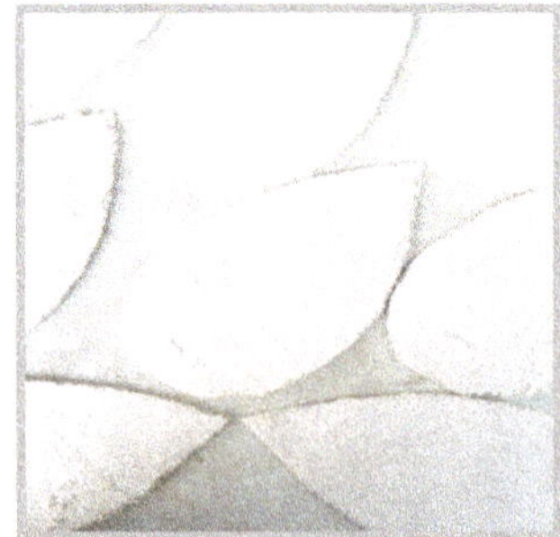

4   Spread another smooth layer of tile adhesive using the trowel on each part and let dry.

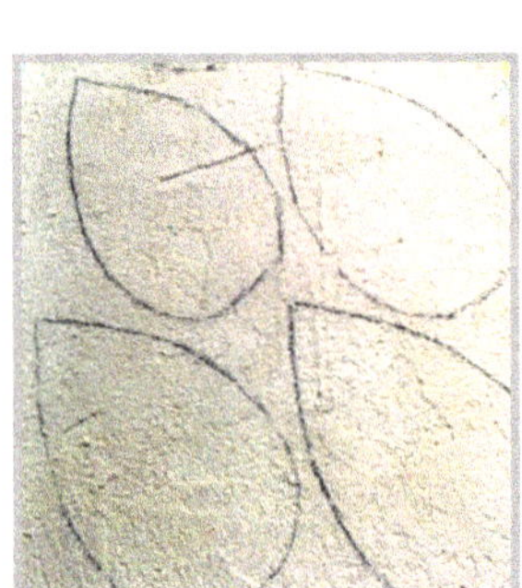

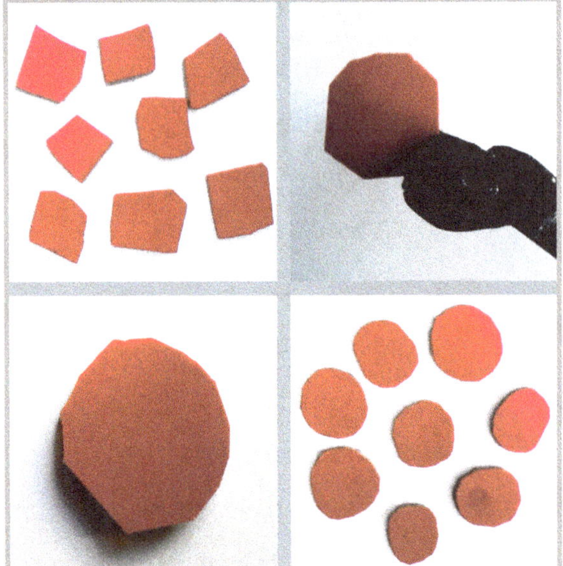

5   The flower center is made of ceramic and glass circles, various sizes.

Preparing the ceramics circles:

- Cut red mosaic to squares in various sizes. It doesn't have to be an accurate shape.

- Cut "bikes" from four edges and round the shape to get a complete circle.

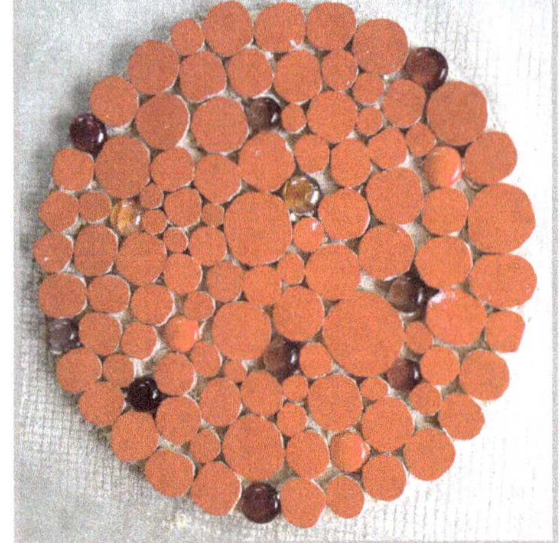

6   Glue the circles next to each other on a round surface with tile adhesive. You can add some round clear glass.

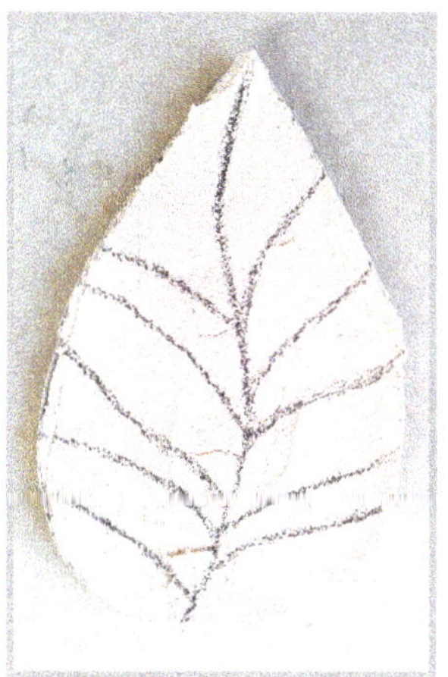 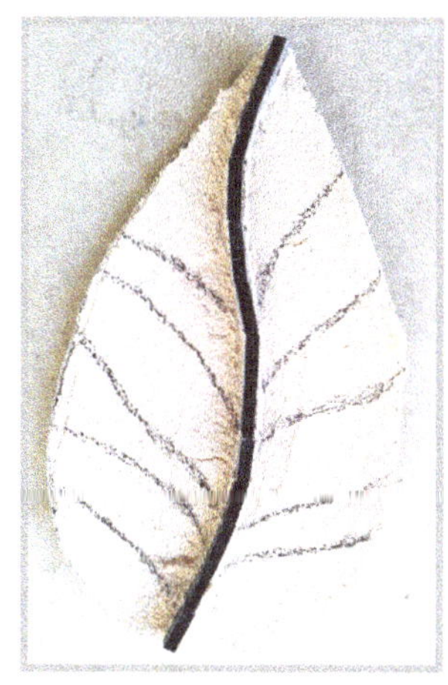 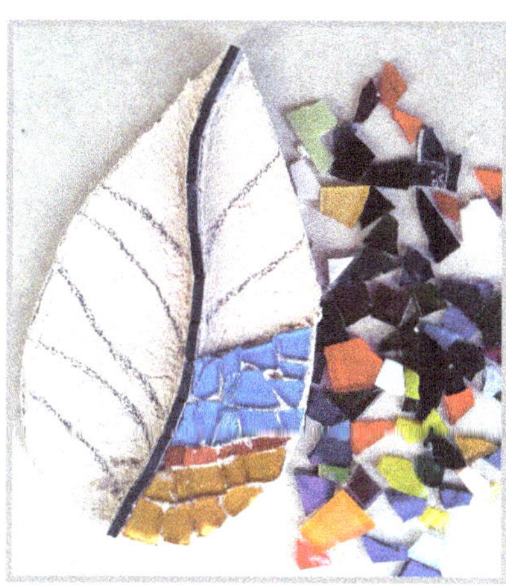

7 Make the leaves: drew with a pencil the vertical center line on each leaf and some dividing lines for separating the colors. The spaces between the lines in each leaf can be in different wide.

8 Cut black glass into thin strips and stick on the midline of the leaf.

9 Prepare the leaves materials: cut stained glass into small pieces, put each color in a separate box.

10 Start pasting the colored stained glass, filling areas as you marked.

11 Keep your work clean from adhesive residue with a screwdriver or a wet wipe at the end of each section.

12 Wait at least 24 hours and grout – see grout instructions. Use black grout for the center and cream for the leaves.

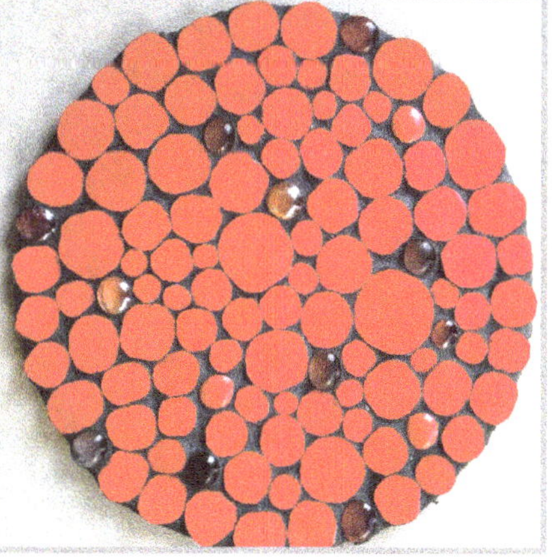 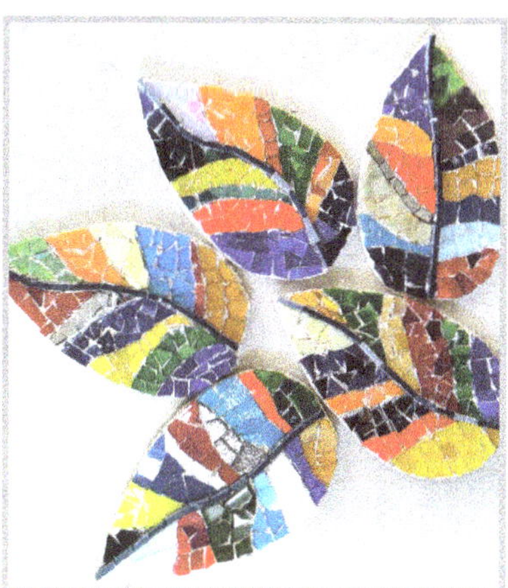

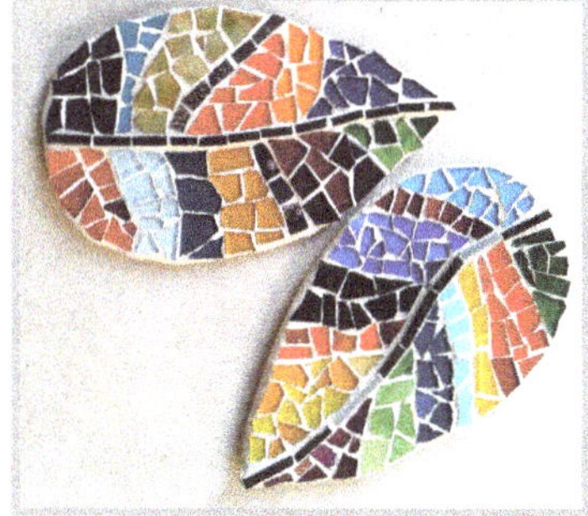

13 Remove the plastic. Start with the flower center piece, spread strong acrylic mastic on the back side, hold and push the pieces into place until they are stuck. Do the same with the leaves, one by one, until you get a perfect flower.

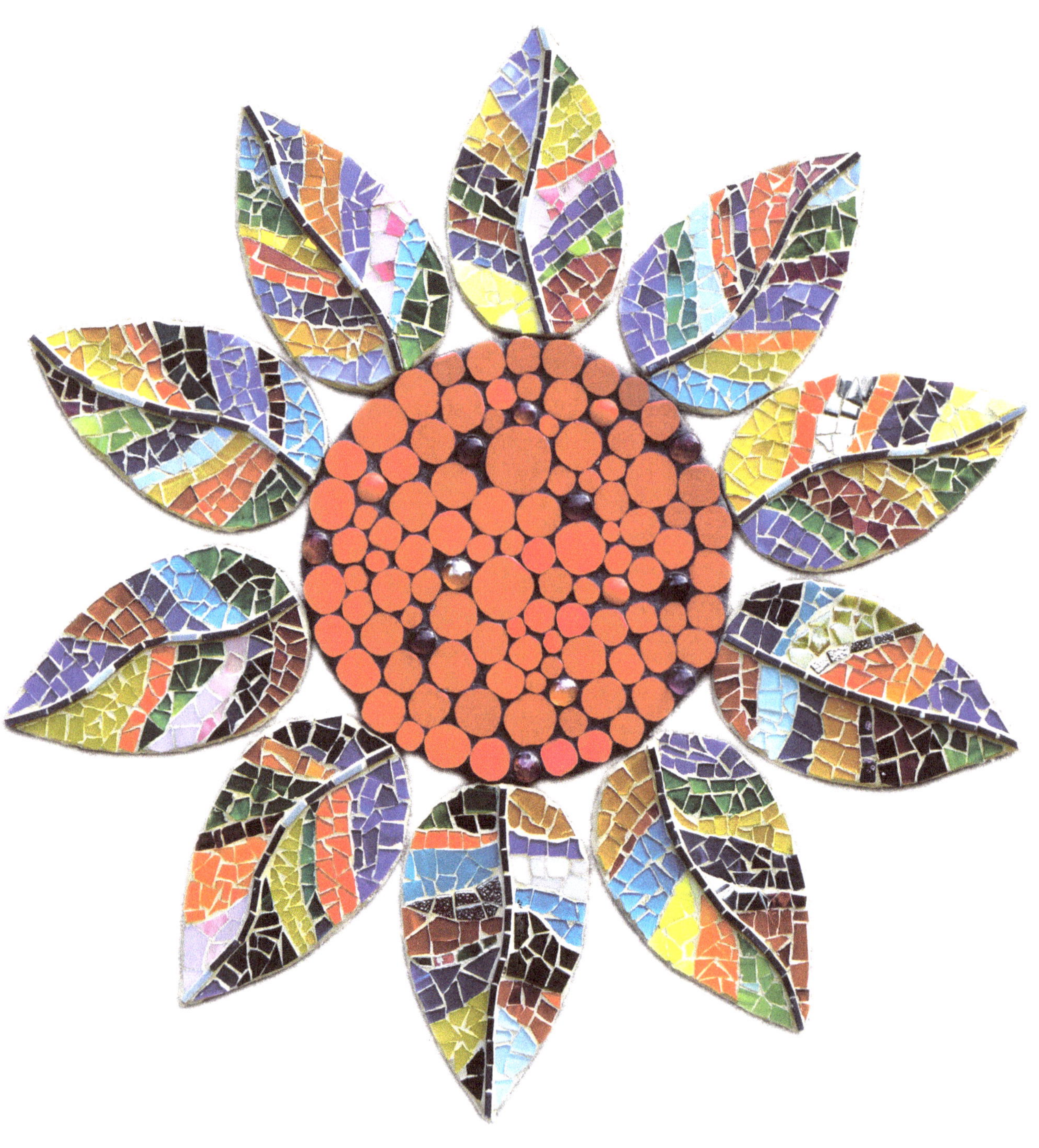

Summary

Thank you, for the trust you have given me, and for taking the time to read the book. In my opinion, the mosaic is a wonderful art. It is a great way to show your creativity and expression. I'm very happy to share my knowledge with you.

In this book, I have focused on mesh mosaic projects. The mesh gives us the flexibility to work and various pasting option – inside and outside walls, stairs, and more options that your imagination can create.

The great advantage of working with mesh is that you can sit comfortably, create the mosaic on your working desk - even the work is very large, and paste it in place when you finish. If you gave up on wall decoration of your house because you thought it would not be stayed comfortable to stand on a ladder and paste stones - no more, there is a solution. Paste the prepared mesh mosaic directly on the wall and enjoy a decorative wall!

Lately, there are a lot of community projects that integrate people from different places. For example, I attended a project that each artist was asked to send a mosaic eye on a fiberglass mesh, and it was connected to a special mosaic art work. The people that participated in the project came from around the world. Each prepared their mosaic eye on mesh base and mailed them in. It was much more practical and convenient than gathering people to a physical place.

We studied two methods for gluing mosaic on mesh. The first one is a direct adhesion, which grouting is made on the wall. The other one is used on a prepared base from tile adhesive and mesh, the grout is used on the mosaic surface itself, and it is pasted, on the wall as ready work.

The mesh work allows us to create complex images with different materials: ceramics, fragments of cups and plates, beads, glass, stones and much more. This is the opportunity to experience working with cups and plates that gives texture and patterns that ceramic don't have by using colored stones and combining them into work. The most important thing to remember is to open your imagination and be creative!

Good luck,

Sigalit Eshet

Students works

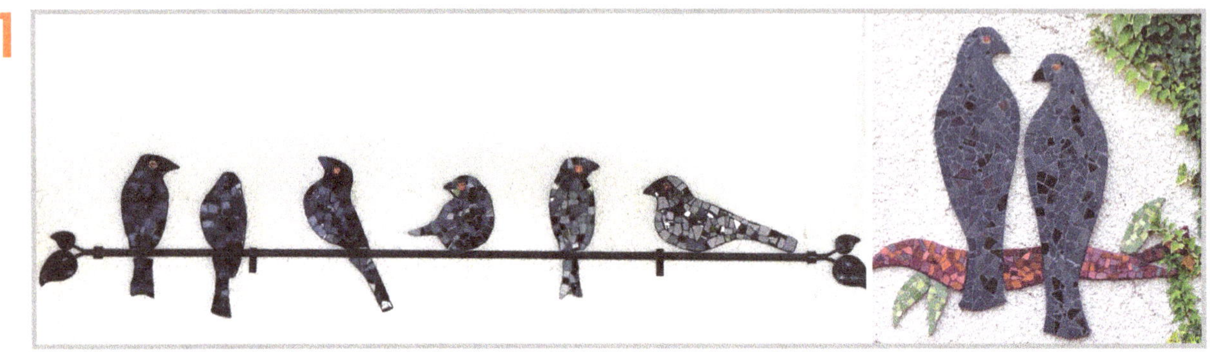

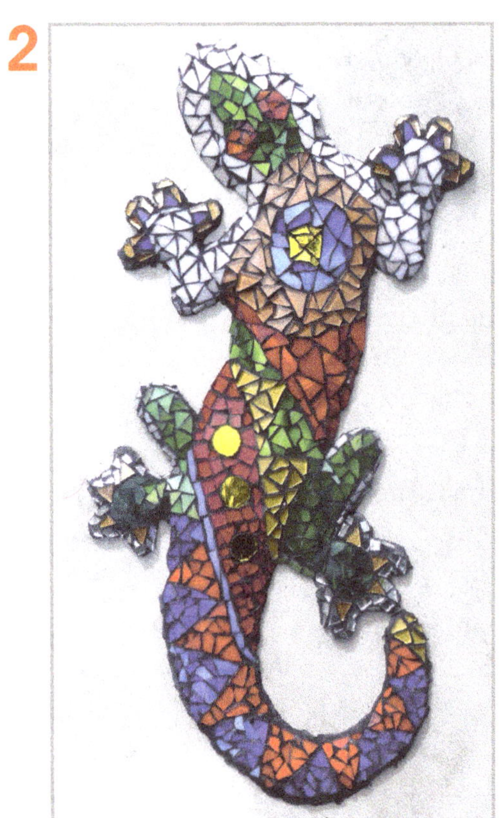

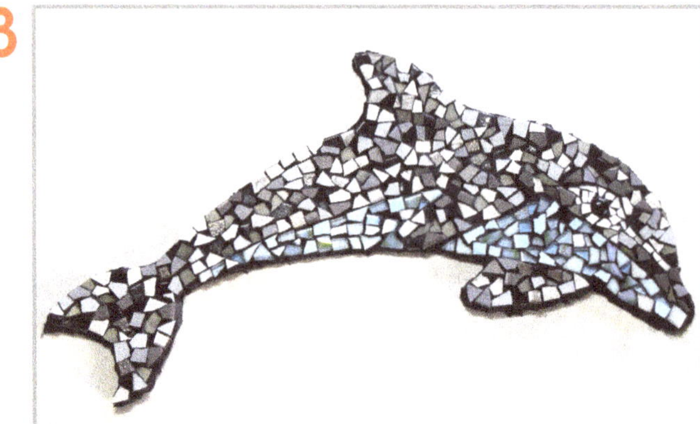

1. Black birds made by Dorit – stained glass on ready mesh base

2. Dalia's Colorful lizard – stained glass on ready mesh base

3. Nava's dolphin – stained glass on ready mesh base

4. Wall decorating strips made by Iris – ceramic tiles, plates, cups and glass on mesh

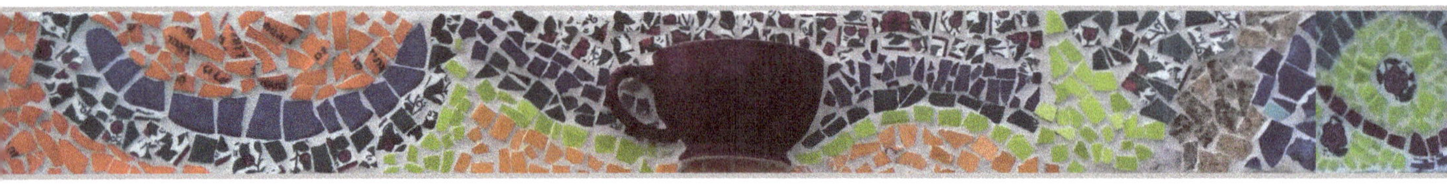

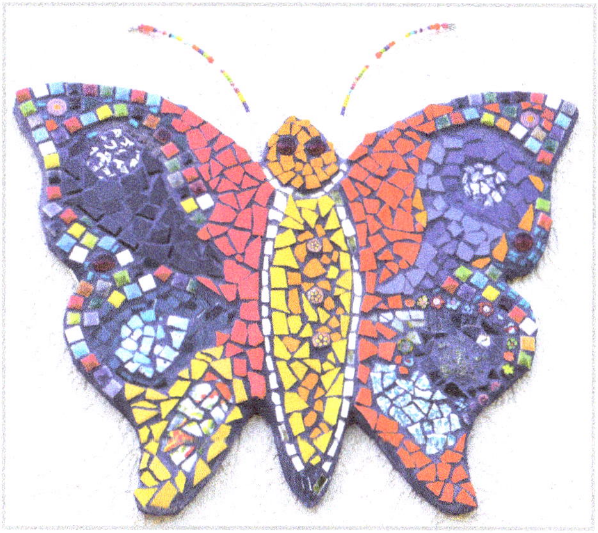

5. Wall decorating strips made by Judith – ceramic, glass nuggets and glass squares on mesh, before hanging and grouting

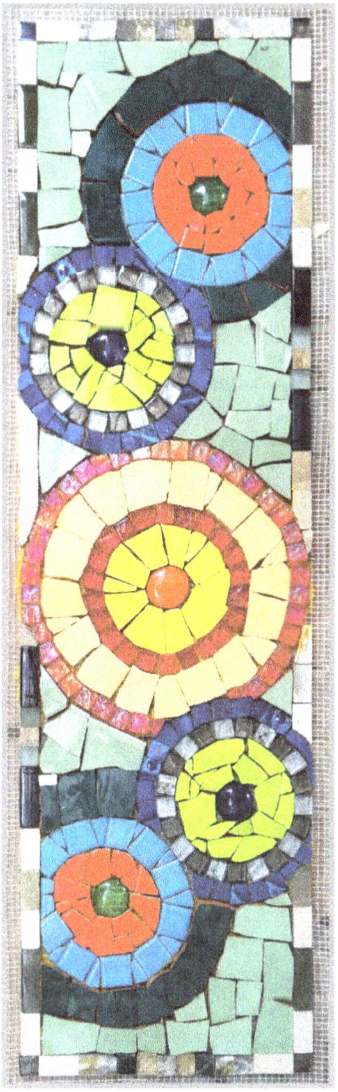

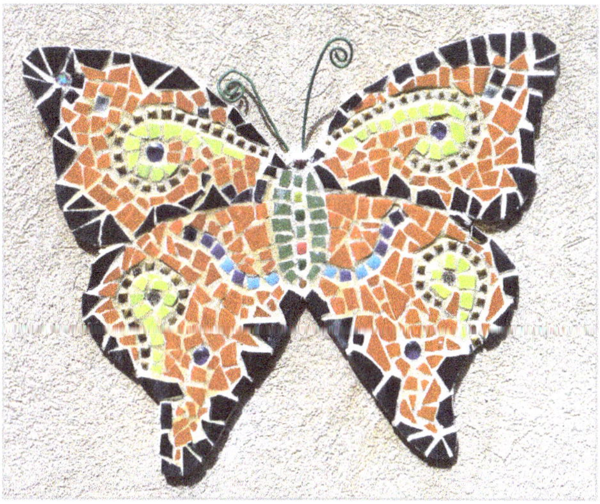

6. Efrat's butterfly – Ceramic tiles on mesh

7. Varda's butterfly – colored stained glass on ready mesh base

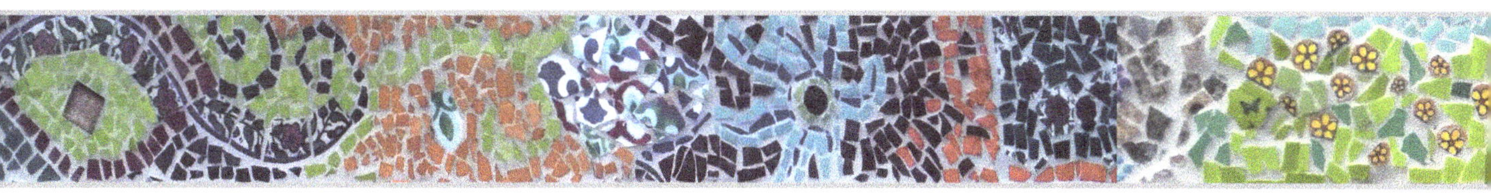

<u>Other e-books from this author on Amazon:</u>

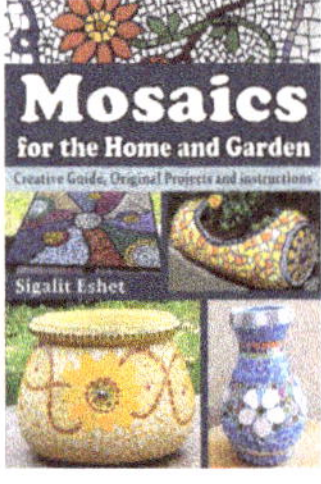 Mosaics for the Home and Garden

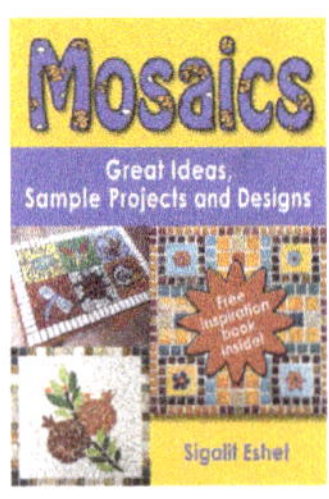 Mosaics: Great Ideas and Projects

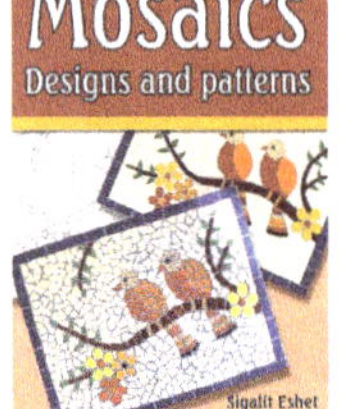 Mosaics - Designs and patterns

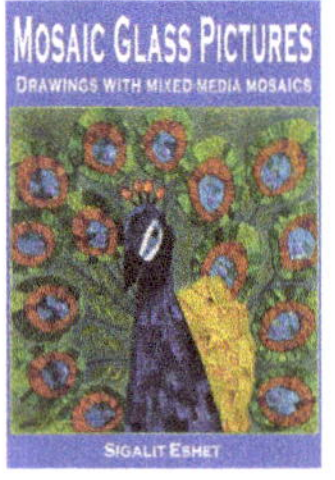 Mosaic Glass Pictures

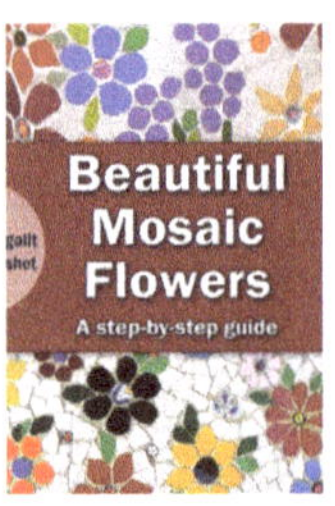 Beautiful Mosaic Flowers

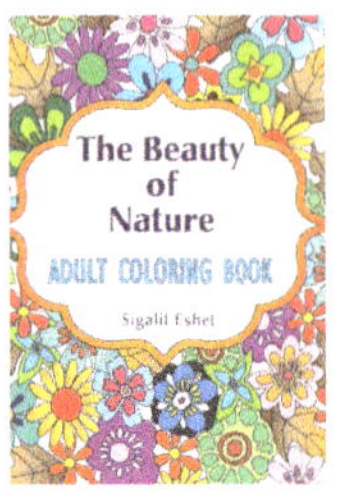 Adult coloring book: The beauty of nature

www.ingramcontent.com/pod-product-compliance
Lightning Source LLC
Chambersburg PA
CBHW080920160726
48000CB00009B/3058